THE ENTREPRENEUR'S GUIDEBOOK

SIMPLE TOOLS TO ENHANCE YOUR ENTREPRENEURIAL JOURNEY

SURESH G. BHARWANI,
CO-AUTHOR: HARSH S. BHARWANI

Notion Press

Old No. 38, New No. 6
McNichols Road, Chetpet
Chennai - 600 031

First Published by Notion Press 2017
Copyright © Suresh G. Bharwani 2017
All Rights Reserved.

ISBN 978-1-946983-51-0

This book has been published with all reasonable efforts taken to make the material error-free after the consent of the author. No part of this book shall be used, reproduced in any manner whatsoever without written permission from the author, except in the case of brief quotations embodied in critical articles and reviews.

The Author of this book is solely responsible and liable for its content including but not limited to the views, representations, descriptions, statements, information, opinions and references ["Content"]. The Content of this book shall not constitute or be construed or deemed to reflect the opinion or expression of the Publisher or Editor. Neither the Publisher nor Editor endorse or approve the Content of this book or guarantee the reliability, accuracy or completeness of the Content published herein and do not make any representations or warranties of any kind, express or implied, including but not limited to the implied warranties of merchantability, fitness for a particular purpose. The Publisher and Editor shall not be liable whatsoever for any errors, omissions, whether such errors or omissions result from negligence, accident, or any other cause or claims for loss or damages of any kind, including without limitation, indirect or consequential loss or damage arising out of use, inability to use, or about the reliability, accuracy or sufficiency of the information contained in this book.

This book is dedicated to my parents,
Shri. Gordhandas Bharwani and Mrs. Lilawati Bharwani.
I seek your blessings.

All proceeds of this book will be donated to Open Seva Education and Health Care foundation an NGO managed by my Wife Mrs. Anisha Bharwani who relentlessly looks after needs of underprivileged children.
I thank her for being my support system.

Contents

Acknowledgements		*vii*
Foreword		*ix*
Introduction		*xi*
1.	5 Types of Entrepreneurs	1
2.	Customer Resonance	8
3.	Mind-sets: Foundation of an Entrepreneur	16
4.	Niche Selection	63
5.	Getting the Business Model Right	98
6.	How to Get Your First 10 Customers	110
Timeline of Suresh G. Bharwani		*122*

ACKNOWLEDGEMENTS

I would like to thank all the individuals who have helped me through my life. It is their contributions that have made my journey memorable and meaningful.

First and foremost I would like to thank my father, *Shri Gordhandas Bharwani*. He was a multifaceted and practical person, a committed householder and a karma yogi. His life was selfless, much like that of a saint who strives for the wellbeing of others.

My mother *Smt. Lilawati Bharwani* was an iron lady, efficiently managing the responsibilities of our lives, homes and our relations at the same time, like an orchestra coordinator. She instilled in me the qualities of quietly seeking wisdom, while going about ones duties.

Dr. *Jaydev*, *yogi*-par-excellence is my guru. He was always there for me - "Anytime and every time", guiding and helping at every step. He understood my strengths and weaknesses, and when I was standing at the cross roads of my life, nobody could have shown me a clearer path. Week after week, during my difficult days, he reminded me, "Take care of yourself."

My wife *Anisha* is one of sharpest women in the world. She is kind, supports me and puts up with all my weaknesses and quirks. She has truly taken good care of me and I am deeply grateful for all that she has done for our family.

My brothers *Nandu* and *Jitu*, have been like pillars of strength and confidence. Our healthy sibling rivalry and mutual respect, gave us a strong culture of discussion and debate, which has kept me on my toes and spurred me to do better.

My sisters *Vimla, Shobha, Hiro* and *Kamloo* have been great inspiration. They have excelled in academics and spirituality and brought those learnings to my life.

Acknowledgements

Bob Pike, the creator of Creative Training Techniques, has been my significant professional teacher-He taught me in two days, how one can make training, learning, meetings, fun, faster and easier. "Ask, not tell" has been his mantra that I have internalised in my life.

"When in doubt, ask", but to whom? He is objective, does not take sides, call a spade a spade and he is none other than *Mr. Vijay Sampath*, who refused to accept a retainership from us, so as to keep our "friendship" pure. He is point blank and frankly tells me, "Suresh, you are wrong."

My sons *Harsh, Avinash* and *Sidharth* are the reflections of my personality, and in their spirit, energy and hopes, I see myself, like looking in a "mirror."

Mr. Zafar Khan, who taught me the fundamentals of advertising, differentiation strategy & helped me to propel my success against giants.

Mrs. Sita Samtani (Principal of *Kamla* High School) who lived the life of a Saint and worked tirelessly for the education of *Sindhi* refugees and whose inspiring life lit the spark of education and training in me.

All my invaluable business partners, who taught me that "win- win" is the only way to do a sustainable business.

And most importantly, the seven lakh students I have interacted with over the years, and whose hopes and aspirations reminded me that keeping our promise of "100% job guarantee" is more important than anything else in the world.

Foreword

I have known *Suresh Bharwani* for two decades. Over the years I have admired him for achieving so much in the face of adversity and challenge. Interacting with him has been a learning experience as his life experiences and entrepreneurial skills are unparalleled.

His path-breaking book is a great contribution to Indian entrepreneurship. It is a wonderfully motivating guide that can explode the entrepreneurial horizons of every smart and ambitious individual, regardless of age or experience.

The book draws on his many noteworthy achievements at Jetking, which he rebuild single-handedly from an "old world" electronics manufacturer, to its position today as one of India's leading technology training companies.

From the business capital of planning, strategy and detailed operations, to the human capital of harnessing personal skills, this book covers the entire spectrum of capabilities required to build a successful business.

This book is recommended not only for the individual seeking entrepreneurial guidance but also serves as a valuable addition to corporate libraries and educational institutions.

- Vijay Sampath

INTRODUCTION

Thank you for owning this book. You just made a great investment for your future. You are in the top 1% of the people who want to take control of their lives, and the fact that you have selected this book tells me you have what it takes to succeed. You are amongst the few who do, versus the many who talk. Research states that 90% of the people who buy a book do not read past the first chapter. However, my belief is that you are in the 10% who will read through the book and take meaningful action to start and scale your business.

I was at an annual CII award function recently, and as I sat in the audience the presenter announced, "The award goes to Jetking. May I invite *Suresh G Bharwani*, Chairman and Managing Director of Jetking to come on stage and receive the award for providing the best skills training in the industry!" This is one of the three awards that I really cherish. As I walked to the stage, my whole life flashed in front of my eyes: how I started my business career, how I failed and how I succeeded again. These flash backs were like a movie where a few events unfolded in slow motion and the rest just zoomed past. I remembered how I had seven imported cars (having one imported car was big back then), and how I had to travel by bus for seven years having lost all my money. My relatives drove past me in big cars. How after successfully selling radios in exhibition my pockets were full of cash, as I went home and how I visited banks every single morning to plead with bank managers to allow payments to be disbursed.

From becoming the most successful radio manufacturer in the country to losing everything and three crores in debt (which is equivalent to 30 to 50 crores of rupees in today's terms), and then becoming the world's largest IT training company. Jetking has trained. Achieving over Rs. 1000 crores in sales, managing over 140 franchises, students contributing over Rs. 70,000 crores to GDP every month in the Indian economy, and most importantly, managing myself. I am humbled that I still have a long way to go. In this book

Introduction

I present to you my journey with over forty years of experience of what it takes to start, scale and make a business successful.

I will not just give you practical stories, tips, tools and techniques to start, scale and make a business successful, but the secrets of how to manage yourself and your relationships as a businessman, because this is more important than anything else by far.

After achieving nirvana, Lord *Buddha* went from village to village to spread his teachings. In one such village, while he was teaching when three friends came along with a blind man. One of the friends spoke to Lord Buddha. "Our friend is blind and we have been trying to convince him that there is light in this world, but he is not convinced. His belief is so strong that although we know there is light, we had to give up."

His friend added, "He says if there is light I want to touch the light. Lord Buddha, how is this possible?"

The third friend then interrupted, "Our blind friend also said that if touching the light is not possible then he wants to hear the light. Tell me, my lord, how is this possible?"

Hearing this, the first friend said, "Our blind friend says if it's not possible to hear the light, he wants to smell it. Is that possible, Lord Buddha? It is very difficult to prove to our friend that there is light because light can only be seen. He also goes and complains to our relatives and villagers that we are trying to prove that he is blind and that he is confident there is no such thing as light. We request you to make him understand that there is light, as he will believe you, Lord Buddha."

Lord Buddha, being the enlightened one, replied, "Why should I make him understand what he doesn't want to understand? Most preachers make the mistake of teaching people what they cannot understand. He doesn't need preaching; what he needs is treatment. I know an excellent *Vaid* (doctors in ancient India). Take your friend to him and see if any treatment is possible."

So the three friends and the blind man go to the Vaid for the treatment. Ten days later the blind man was able to see. He could not believe himself and wanted to thank Lord *Buddha* for restoring his vision. But Lord Buddha had left that village by then and was four to five villages ahead. The man was determined to find Lord Buddha and thank him. After a few days of searching, the blind man (who wasn't blind anymore) found Lord *Buddha* and fell at his feet and said, "I was wrong Lord Buddha, there is light."

Lord *Buddha* smiled and replied, "You were wrong, but the fact that you didn't listen to anyone helped you get your eyesight back. If you had listened to your friends, then you would have never got your eyesight back."

The moral of the story is that when reading this book, read it with a curious mind. Curiosity is the starting point of emotion for any learning. A child absorbs information at lightning speed because he is curious about everything. This state of being curious will help you succeed more than anything else.

This book is made up of three parts. Part one is about the mind-set required to start a business. Mind-sets are like a foundation. Just like a strong building or tree requires a strong foundation, to be a successful entrepreneur, you need to understand the mind-set of successful entrepreneurs. This is not something that I have invented. It is something that I have learnt from my mentors, books, and experience over the period of the past forty years. You will have to develop these mind-sets at the end of the day if you want to establish a successful business. If your business is not performing as per your plan, it is because you have not developed the required mind-set.

Part two requires that you learn everything about what I do to find the right target market or niches that will pay you even before you invest anything in the business. One of the toughest things for a human being to do is to get another human being to take out money from their wallet and give it to you. 90% of businessman or entrepreneurs fail in this phase of business.

Part three is about scaling a business. When you have a successful business model, the toughest part is knowing how to scale the business. I have personally scaled my business through franchising, but there are other models of scaling, like building software, partnerships, and organic growth.

INTRODUCTION

I urge you to go through the book at least two to three times to really understand it. Repetition is the mother of skills. So, the more you repeat it, the better it will go into your subconscious mind.

As a businessman and a human being, there were lots of ups and down that I went through in life. I was raised in a poor family. My mother passed away, suffering from disease for almost after five years. I was extremely close to her, and every day when I come back from the office, I used to go to her room and spend half an hour with her. My father passed away when I was just twenty-eight. I was totally lost and didn't know what to do, as it was my turn to take responsibility of the house. My youngest brother suddenly died at the young age of 45. I got into debt, had to sell all my shops and cars, travel for seven years in a bus, with the support of the whole family and little money in my pocket. My relatives deserted me at the time when I needed them the most. I am embarrassed to say that there was a man in our building who owned a car and had his office near my office. I used to watch from my window waiting for him to come down, and as soon as he came down, I used to rush down, pretending that I had just come down and met him coincidently. I would leave for my office in his car (that didn't work out in the long-run). My younger brother had a neuro degenerative disease – the Parkinson's disease (which still doesn't have a cure). I also had health issues like enlarged prostate, high blood pressure, and piles. For years I had to deal with piles. If you have gone through physical pain for a long period of time, you will realise it is very difficult to cope with. A person cannot think about anything else and wants to just get rid of the physical pain.

I will tell you secrets that helped me recover and come back stronger than before. It is to the point that today all my sons live with me. Nine of us have lunch and dinner together, I built the world's largest IT training company, and I eliminated my piles. Most things don't affect me as much as it used to now.

I read an interview of *Subramaniam Ramadorai* (ex-vice chairman of TCS), who said that India has become a paper degree country. People over here give more value to the degree even if it did not get them a job. It is important to make them realise that doing something with their own hands is also important and can fetch them a job. I agree with what he says. If a student focuses on training and education to improve his skills, he will not require the degree. Many successful businessmen are high school dropouts. It's not to say you don't need to study, but today's education is not relevant to the skills that are required to be successful in life.

If you really want to grow in your business and personal life, you have to leave your comfort zone. You will find that the only time you grow is when you are outside your comfort zone. If you go back and look at your past and think about the times where you have grown, you can see that you were out of your comfort zone. Think about how you build your muscles. Imagine that you are in a gym working on your biceps and you have to do ten curls. Which is the most difficult one to do? Number 10, right? Which will give you all the growth? Number 12! When you are getting the most tired and you are about to give up and your trainer tells you to do two more, you say "no" and he shouts at you to "DO IT." When you do it, that's when you will grow. Similarly, your business muscles, your relationship muscles, and your learning muscles will grow only when you get out of your comfort zone. I will tell you to do exercises at the end of each chapter that will push you out of your comfort zone and help you grow in various aspects of life. Not doing the exercise is like getting Rs. 100 crores and never using it. I urge you to take out half an hour every day and do these exercises.

Over the past forty years I have found that the foundations of success are not obvious and often counter-intuitive.

Do you know which the tallest building in the world was for a long time? It was the Petronas tower in Malaysia (it still exists, but it's not the tallest anymore. While writing this book, it was the BurjKhalifa). The height is approx. 1438 feet. When you see the tower you go, "Wow, that's a beautiful tower." Did you know that to build such a tower it took a foundation of about 390 feet below the ground? It is very counter-intuitive to think that you must first dig a hole and build down before you can build up.

It is intuitive to focus on your own needs and be counter-intuitive to put yourself aside and focus on other people's needs. It's intuitive to convince people to buy what you have, but counter-intuitive to ask people what their needs are. Understand their needs and design a product according to their needs, and then tell them to buy it.

It is intuitive to be the smart one, talk about yourself and your ideas, but it is counter-intuitive to let other people be the smart ones. It is intuitive to pursue an idea that you like for thirty years, spend all your money on it and think this is the best idea in the world. It is counter-intuitive to understand what the market wants and give them that product and test it out to see how scalable it can be.

It is intuitive to consume and feel good now, like the feeling junk food, sugar, and credit cards give you. It is counter-intuitive to save, invest and let your investments give you compounded returns over a period of five to ten years.

It is intuitive to multi-task (focusing on too many things at once), and counter-intuitive to focus on one task, bring it to completion and then move on to the next task.

It is intuitive to do everything in your business well. It is counter-intuitive to do one thing way better than 'well' and not worry about other aspects as much (maybe outsource, delegate, etc.)

It is intuitive to grab every opportunity that comes your way. It is counter-intuitive to let all of those opportunities go by and not get distracted by them.

It is intuitive to let losses, problems, situations, and things that go wrong affect you emotionally and destabilise you. It is counter-intuitive to think all these things will help you learn and grow to the next level.

It is intuitive to work harder if you're not getting results. It is counter-intuitive to take a break, relax for a bit and then come back and work on it.

Let me narrate to you the story of the King of Persia and his beautiful talking bird. He was very fond of this bird and considered it valuable and important to him and his kingdom. He kept it locked in a golden cage. The bird retained most of its beauty but ceased learning new stories and songs to tell the king. Even so, because of its beautiful voice and pleasing manners, the king never became bored because of the fact that it could still talk.

After few years, matters of state took the king to the bird's homeland. He told the bird where he was going and asked if there was anything he could do for the bird in return for its many years of service to him. The bird responded enthusiastically, asking to be taken along on the journey. The king would not agree, fearing that the bird would be stolen or would escape.

The bird then asked the king if he would take a message to its family. The king readily agreed. The bird then asked the king to tell his family that he was captured and kept in a cage for the king's pleasure. Further, the bird requested the king to ask it's family how he could flourish while being a prisoner in a cage. The king travelled to the bird's homeland and went into the jungle in search of the bird's family, mindful of his promise.

After some days, he found the family and relayed the bird's message. Upon hearing of the bird's captivity and the message, the bird's family fell off the tree and onto ground as if dead. The sight of the dead birds horrified the king. When he returned to his kingdom, as gently as possible he informed his captive bird of what had transpired in the jungle.

Upon hearing the story, the bird immediately fell on the floor of its cage. The king assumed that the shock of hearing such a sad story had killed the bird. He carefully opened the cage, removed the bird, and gently placed it on the tables as he prepared for its burial. As soon as the king's hands were off the bird, the bird flew out the window, free from the prison of the cage.

The king angrily demanded that the bird explain these events. The bird calmly said, "My family was giving you a message for me. In response to my question of how I could continue to flourish while imprisoned in this cage, they showed me that the way to freedom was to drop dead to the circumstances that had created the boundaries of my imprisonment. Only by 'dying' to the current situation could I find freedom." To take full advantage of this book, you have to die to your current situation that has imprisoned you in the golden cage. You have to let go of your fears, frustrations and failures. These are the events of your past. Have faith in the ideas presented, they will help you grow.

Introduction

I am extremely excited to write this book and share the secrets of success. Read this book at least three times to get the full value out of it. I have read my mentor Bob Pike's book at least forty times and I keep referring to it from time to time. When I refer to it after a couple of months and I read one page, that same page gives me a different perspective. I would like your feedback on this book. If you want help with implementing anything written in this book, email me at *support@lifeguarantee.org* and we will help you with it.

CHAPTER 1

5 Types of Entrepreneurs

I recently heard of a statistic stating that within five years of starting up, 50% of businesses shut down and within the next ten years only 33% survive. That means that only fifteen out of 100 companies succeed. If you see the Fortune 100 list, my guess is that only a handful of companies like GE have been able to survive the list over the last 100 years. The rest of the companies have either shut shop or declined in revenues.

I believe that an entrepreneur has a tough life. He has to manage his people, pay salaries on time, make sure he has paid his taxes, pay rent on time, and change according to market conditions. If he starts making handsome profits, suddenly family members and friends who never kept in touch start asking for favours and some government departments also come knocking to take their share. Everyone expects the entrepreneur to treat each department equally. He has to keep his ego, desire, and assumption on the side and satisfy his customer. Competition is ready to copy each and every successful idea executed by the entrepreneur.

He has to discipline himself since there is no one above him, work with his belief system about possibilities, survive and thrive in negative circumstances, change his people's negative mind-sets, act confident and positive even if there are huge frustrations inside his body and mind, keep adapting to changes and advances in technology, recruit the right staff, manage financial constraints, maintain a balance between personal and business life, keep health in check and not feel appreciated.

Writing down your feelings help in identifying them and that in turn helps in controlling them. The secret to identifying the true issue is to express it in one sentence comprising about ten words. Describe each of your frustrations in one sentence.

_____
_____
_____
_____
_____
_____

Wiki.com lists the top five challenges of an entrepreneur as:
1. Inadequate finance
2. High cost of raw materials and other inputs
3. Unfavourable market conditions
4. Unreliable supply of raw materials, power, labour, etc.
5. Complex rules, regulations, procedures laid down by the government.

I am surrounded by entrepreneurs all the time and recently one of my relatives died. He was an extremely successful entrepreneur, and one of the wealthiest persons in my family. Everyone respected him, he had helped people in need. He was from a small town and when he became successful he helped many people in his village. I was extremely disappointed to see that his sons were fighting over his wealth. An entrepreneur also has to deal with family fights and partnerships gone sour, which is increasingly growing in recent times.

Recently I was driving through the world-famous shopping district Linking Road in *Bandra* (a suburb of Mumbai) and it was surprising to see shops opening and shutting down every year. Ten years ago, shops used to last for at least five years. Today I see shops opening and shutting every six months. I can only imagine the loss the entrepreneur goes through. The entrepreneur faces not only financial losses, but mental and emotional stress as well.

Twenty years ago, when I was in debt and my house was about to be auctioned by banks, I was in tears. My mother shouted at me, telling me that I had destroyed her husband's (my father's) wealth and that I had no right to do so. This was the turning point in my life.

Over a period of time, I have identified five types of entrepreneurs:

1. The Fearful Professional

During my training with hundreds of entrepreneurs I always ask them what motivates them, and they come up with stuff like having 100 crores in the bank, owning a Ferrari, and living in a penthouse. In my experience (and researchers have also proven this) human beings are motivated twice as much by fear/pain than by pleasure. People will do more to save themselves from losing what they already have than take risks and possibly gain three times as much (or even more).

This, by far, is the biggest reason most people don't start a new business and stay stuck in their current job or misery. The pleasure has a possibility of beating the current pain 100 times over. Still, most people will be ruled by fear and prefer to stay in their comfort zone. Most people will moan about how their life sucks and that they want control over it. They will even grow old doing a job they might not like, but very few will actually take steps to become an entrepreneur. I have spoken with brilliant people from IIT, IIM and other world-class institutions. They are somehow unable to start a business on their own. However, this trend is fast changing. If you can relate with this, I would urge you to think differently.

Imagine how your life will turn out if you continue to do what you're currently doing. Fifteen years down the line, how will you feel about your life? If you continue to do what you're currently doing, you will get the same results you've always got.

2. The Estimated Entrepreneur

There are a number of people who start their business with a lot of excitement and pomp. They take huge loans from banks. They believe that their business will be the next big app in the market, yet six months down the line they start losing steam.

It is not what they imagined. The forest looks different from the plane and very different when you are actually standing in the middle of it. When they start, these entrepreneurs do what is called 'emotional estimation'. Before the business has started they start calculating the revenues and the profits they are likely to earn. Then they start thinking about all the pleasure they will have once they have the estimated cash in their bank. The kind of car they will buy, the kind of house they will move into, and all the respect they will get. Based on this estimation they put all the money they have plus all the loans they can possibly get into the business. There is no assessment of reality. I learnt this lesson the hard way in one of my business ventures when I estimated the profit before the start of the business. After six months to a year, reality dawns upon them and suddenly it strikes that the market has changed and the demand for the product has reduced, or a better product/service/software has come into the market. Competition for their product has increased and the product has become a commodity; in fact, a big MNC is selling the product for $1/10^{th}$ the price. Now they are stuck with the loan, and the rising interest cost. They reach a point where they are fed up of this whole failure.

Not only financial losses, but mental and emotional stress as well starts taking their toll. Their confidence takes a huge hit. They sell everything they have and promise never to become an entrepreneur ever again. Ever since that day, they say entrepreneurship cannot be learnt, it is something that you either have or you don't.

3. The Society Conditioned Professional

The third kind is someone who doesn't believe that he/she can become a successful entrepreneur. This is because the only way they have learnt to become financially independent is to do a job. Doing a job is not necessarily good or bad. However, if you want to take control of your life and live a life of freedom, entrepreneurship is something that you must explore. Social conditioning plays a big role with this kind of person. They are surrounded by people doing jobs, so they can't even imagine doing something different. They have been taught that they must become a doctor or an engineer and get a safe job in either the government sector or an MNC. Get married, have children, and teach their children to be ready for the job market. They continue with this life style even if their salary is really low, they dislike going to work every morning and possibly hate their bosses.

4. The Average Entrepreneur

The fourth kind of person is someone who is already an entrepreneur, and has achieved success in business. This person was making money at the start and therefore has lasted so far. But inflation has stepped in. They are only, what I call, surviving. Rents have sky rocketed and salaries have risen. Fifty or more people are selling the same product at half the price. As the days pass by they are getting more and more stressed out. They start thinking about what made them successful, then try to implement that all over again. The problem with this approach is that the market has changed considerably. Secondly, at different stages of a business, different mind-sets and strategies need to be used. So, for a start-up the strategy is completely different than business which has reached a million dollars in revenues (Rs. 6 crores).

Scaling a million dollars to 10 million dollars in revenues, an entirely different mind-set is required. And from 10 million dollars to a billion dollars, again a completely different mind-set is required.

Tony Robbins states that only 10% of humans actually go ahead and achieve the success they dream of. The only reason most people don't become successful is because they don't know what they want, and even if they do, they don't get proper guidance, so they get lost along the way. Despite these setbacks some entrepreneurs are extremely successful from a very early age.

5. The Superstar Entrepreneur

This is the fifth category of entrepreneur, and it is what I call the 'superstar entrepreneur'. This list of entrepreneurs includes *Mark Zuckerberg* of Facebook, *Bill Gates* of Microsoft, *Sam Walton* of Walmart, *Sunil Bharti Mittal* of Airtel, *Kishor Biyani* of Future Group, *Jeff Bezos* of Amazon, *Larry Page* of Google and so on.

Now, here is an opportunity you must not miss. The technology needed to become a superstar entrepreneur has advanced to a level which is unimaginable. Just like we have advanced in medicine, computers, phones, building roads and almost every technology that exists, we must realise that success technology to help entrepreneurs become successful has advanced. I have spent my life studying, implementing and teaching these systems, and in this book I am presenting to you the five secrets of becoming a superstar entrepreneur.

A few years ago, you needed considerable infrastructure to become an entrepreneur. Just to form a company you had to bribe officers. Today you can form a company with just the click of a button. You don't need to set up a physical infrastructure to start a business. You can set up a website and your business is started. You don't need to hire people and pay them a monthly salary. You can outsource a project to people anywhere in the world. At the end of the project you pay the person for the services and that's it. You don't even need to be physically present to run a business, as the internet does everything for you. Come to think of it, you don't even need a website anymore. If you have heard about concepts like Amazon and Flipkart marketplace, you just tie-up with these e-commerce organisations and they do everything for you. Right from shipping and customer service to collecting payments, logistics and marketing everything is taken care of. The speed at which the market is changing is phenomenal.

Today, eighteen-year-olds become billionaires in 2–3 years. Technologies like the iPhone, Facebook, Google, Instagram, and LinkedIn have changed the way we understand, interact and deal with customers.

Exercise:

This chapter described the different types of entrepreneurs. Before you proceed, it is important that you determine the category of entrepreneur you fall under. Read the various categories of entrepreneurs again and identify the traits that you find in yourself. Which category of entrepreneur do you belong to? What traits of the category do you demonstrate?

_____
_____
_____
_____
_____
_____

The Start- Stop – Continue tool helps you to develop an action plan based on your learnings from this chapter. In sentences comprising not more than ten words each, write down the three things that you will:

Start _____
_____
_____

Stop _____
_____
_____

Continue _____
_____
_____

CHAPTER 2

CUSTOMER RESONANCE

The famous marketer Don Growler spoke about a research done by a company where if a company wanted to reach every American household, it has to spend $350 million…a month! This is crazy. No matter how much you spend on newspaper advertisements, TV or online marketing, you will never be able to reach all of your target segments. You need to have customer resonance.

After spending over forty years in marketing and sales, I have realised the real term for marketing. It is called "customer resonance."

What does resonance mean?

According to dictionary.com, resonance is:

Acoustics intensification and prolongation of sound, especially of a musical tone, produced by sympathetic vibration.

Physics: Sound produced by a body vibrating in sympathy with a neighbouring source of sound.

If you ring the bell in a temple, the sound doesn't stop instantly; it resonates for five to seven seconds. Similarly, a product or service needs to be such that it resonates amongst your target audience so that people start using your product or service more due to one customer talking about it to another.

Imagine someone comes to you one morning and tells you that there are 1000 Mercedes available for 100,000 each, and to tell all your friends and relatives to buy. How fast will it take to sell 1000 cars?

How much will he have to spend on advertising? Nothing. Think about creating a product like that.

When I started my training institute, I sold the course for a price of 12,000. I could enrol only five students in two months. I was at loss and did not know what to do. Then one of my consultants advised me to reduce the price by half. In two months I had 160 students. And the rest is history.

So how do you get one customer talking about your product or service to another customer?

When I was a child, I used to talk to my brother about taking a rupee from one crore people and becoming a *crorepati*. Then as I matured, I realised something different. I realised that if I give something worth Rs. 100 and charge Rs. 10, customer resonance will happen. By giving something of so much value, the customer has no choice but to spread the news about how awesome your product or service is!

Now, the question is what is value, and how do you provide dissappropriate value to customers?

Google search defines value as, "The regard that something is held to deserve; the importance, worth, or usefulness of something."

As I give you the history of human evolution, you will start to realise that value is different for different people. What I consider to be of value might be of no value to you, and vice versa. To a poor man, two meals a day is extremely valuable and he will work and slog the whole day to get those meals. However, for a billionaire, food might not be as valuable as, say, acquiring the next big business. Value also changes over time. To really understand what value is, you must understand the pain and frustrations of your customer at that point in time.

I have met, trained, spoken to and studied more than 1,000 entrepreneurs. One of the biggest reasons why most entrepreneurs fail is that they go after their passion and not the needs of the customer. I am not referring to the market; I am referring to the customer because the market is made up of customers. And if your customer loves you, your market will love you.

I have realised that compassion is the most profitable emotion. You must have read the book 7 Habits of Highly Effective People by Stephen Covey.

One of the habits he states is, 'Seek first to understand then be understood'. I was speaking to one of the top consultants in India, and he was saying the only reason he gets paid such high fees is because he seeks to understand his customer more than anybody else. Have you ever fallen in love with someone and reached a point so deep that you start to understand the other person without the person even speaking a word? Falling in love with your customer is the key.

Now, how do we understand the customer better? By understanding the pain and frustrations of a customer. One of the definitions of an entrepreneur that has been extremely useful to me is that entrepreneurs are problem solvers. You are being paid to solve a problem. If you come with this mind-set, you will never fail as an entrepreneur. The biggest problem in understanding another human being is that you have to keep your own ego, desires, mind-sets, and assumptions in check and give 100% of your attention to understanding the pain of your customer.

You don't need to master sales. You don't need to master accounts.

You don't need to master human resources. You don't need to master quality.

You should be able to solve the problem for your customer. I'm not saying you shouldn't do any of the above, but if you really understand the pain and frustration of the customer and what the customer wants, then all of the above can be done by employees or outsourced, and you will be a rich man.

In one of my training programmes, a participant asked me why, even though he understood his customers well, he still didn't make a lot of money.

Now, trying to understand the customer because you want to make money and really understanding the pains and frustration of your customer because you want to solve his problems are two different things. With the latter, being paid will happen automatically.

If you understand your customer's problem better than the customer does, he will believe you can solve his problem.

In everything that I have done I have kept my thinking aside and understood my customer (i.e. my students, franchisees, recruiters and my staff members). Before putting out anything and everything in the field, I first took feedback from samples of my customers. Based on the feedback, I modified it and put it out in the market. I start my visit to my business partner's centre with a prayer to Lord *Ganesh* (ask feedback from God!). We have idols of Lord *Ganesh* installed in each centre. I then go directly to the training rooms and take feedback from students. Next, I meet all employees of the centre and ask for their feedback. Then I meet the business partners and ask them for feedback. I repeat this process over and over with all my business partners. I also visit recruiters and repeat the process. I ask them to complete the statement "I will like Jetking more if ..." This activity really tells me what improvements need to be done. After visiting ten centers, I know exactly what my customer is looking for, and I make decisions accordingly. People say Jetking is creative and innovative. If you listen to your customers and change according to their needs, then people will start calling you creative and innovative. Most of my major innovations have come from customer feedback. Like the 100% job guarantee, focusing on only one product, the franchise model, Yoga and Smartrain. This resulted in a growth rate of 60% year on year for four years. So go ahead and understand your customer's pain and frustration.

Different Eras

To understand the pain and frustration of your customer, you must understand how we have evolved since the start of mankind. Stephen Covey explains this beautifully in his book The 8th Habit.

The first era for humans was called the hunter-gatherer era, where humans hunted and foraged for a living. For millions of years, humans survived on hunting animals and gathering fruits and vegetables. They got up in the morning, grabbed their hunting equipment and went hunting. They didn't know whether they would get their food by evening. Imagine for a moment that you have stepped back in time and are a hunter and gatherer of food. Each day you go out with a bow and arrow or stones and sticks to gather food for your family. That's all you've ever known, seen and done to survive. Now imagine someone comes up to you and tries to persuade you to become what he calls a 'farmer'. What do you think your response would be?

You see him go out and scratch the earth and throw little seeds into the ground, and you see nothing; you see him watering the soil and removing weeds and still you see nothing. But eventually you see a great harvest. You notice his yield as a farmer is fifty times greater than yours as a hunter-gatherer, and you are considered to be one of the best. What would you do? You would likely say to yourself, "Even if I wanted to, I couldn't do that. I don't have the skills and I don't have the tools!" You just wouldn't know how that would work.

Now the farmer is so productive that you see him making enough money to send his kids to school and provide them with great opportunities. You are barely surviving. Little by little, you are drawn to go through the intense learning process of becoming a farmer. You raise your children and grandchildren as farmers. That's exactly what happened in our early history. There was downsizing of hunter-gatherers by over 90 percent; they lost their jobs. Several generations pass, and along comes the Industrial Age. People build factories and learn specialisation, delegation and scalability. They learn how to take raw materials through an assembly line with very high levels of efficiency. The productivity of the Industrial Age goes up to fifty times over the family farm. Now if you were a farmer producing fifty times more than hunters-gatherers and all of a sudden you see an industrial factory rise up and start out-producing the family farm by fifty times, what would you say? You might be jealous, even threatened. But what would you need to be a player in the Industrial Age? You would need a completely new skillset and tool-set. More importantly, you would need a new mind-set - a new way of thinking. The fact is that the factory of the Industrial Age produced fifty times more than the family farm, and over time, 90 percent of the farmers were downsized. Those who survived in farming took the Industrial Age concept and created industrialised farms. Today, only 3 percent of the population in the United States are farmers, and they produce most of the food for the entire country and much of the world. Do you believe that the information/ Knowledge Worker Age we are in will out-produce the Industrial Age fifty times? I believe it has. We're just barely beginning to see it. It will out-produce it not twice, not three or ten times, but fifty times. *Nathan Myhrvold*, former Chief Technology Officer of Microsoft, puts it this way: "The top software developers are more productive than average software developers not by a factor of 10X or 100X or even 1000X, but by 10,000X."

Now what has this got to do with understanding customer needs?

As we have progressed in each era, the value that a customer sees has become more intangible. That means you cannot see, feel, or hear what humans perceive as value, unlike the manufacturing era where you could assess the quality of the product with your senses.

Although everything around us has evolved, our brains are still in the hunter-gatherer era. We are still 99% chimp and 1% human. Most of our decisions are still irrational, and we cover it with logic.

Until the industrial era, the value of a commodity was quite visible. For example, if you wanted to buy a product you could measure the quality by seeing it. Today in the knowledge era, value is invisible, which means the quality of the product cannot be judged by the five senses. You have to go to a whole new level to understand what customers' values are.

To help understand what a customers' values, you must understand his pain points, his challenges, his goals and his aspirations. So either you help him achieve his goals and aspirations, or you help him get rid of his problems.

You must ask questions to find the pain and frustrations of your customer. One of the easiest ways to understand a customer is to build rapport and ask them what their biggest pain and frustrations are that you can help solve. Another question that has been extremely useful to me is to ask my customer what their one-year goal is , listen with extreme compassion, and then help them achieve that goal.

You must fall in love with your customer, not your product.

Exercise:

Being an entrepreneur is all about providing a solution to alleviate the pain faced by the customers. To provide a solution, you need to have a good understanding of their pain. Speak with five of your close friends or relatives and ask them what their biggest pain or frustration is, and make a promise to solve their problem if it's within your capacity. Describe each pain or frustration in one sentence comprising ten words.

_____
_____
_____
_____

What was their feedback once you understood their pain and frustration?
_____
_____
_____
_____

What was their feedback once you solved their pain and frustration?

_____
_____
_____
_____

Have you thought of a business idea to start off with? (If not, don't worry, as by the end of the next chapter you will have one. And not just any business idea, a very profitable business idea!)

_____
_____
_____

Understanding your customers' need is the crucial activity that makes or breaks a business. Based on what you have learnt today, to understand your customers' need, what will you:

Start _____
_____
_____

Stop _____
_____
_____

Continue _____
_____
_____

CHAPTER 3

MIND-SETS: FOUNDATION OF AN ENTREPRENEUR

1. What is that One thing you need to become a successful entrepreneur?

By now you know what value is and the questions to ask to understand value. Let's understand the mind-set first, before we get into the mind-set of an entrepreneur. We must understand what a mind-set is all about.

Definition of mind-set

Established set of attitudes held by someone.
1. An inclination or a habit.
2. A habitual or a characteristic mental attitude that determines how you will interpret and respond to situations.

Mind-sets are like the roots of a tree. Roots are the foundation on which trees are built. The deeper and stronger the roots, the stronger will be the tree. In the event of a thunderstorm, the stronger the roots, the better are the chances of the tree surviving. Similarly, having the right mind-set is the key to starting and scaling a successful business.

If you follow this framework, your chances of success increases by 80%. The remaining

20% will depend on how much disciplined action you take to achieve the results.

A young Harvard dropout unconsciously hit on this model and changed the course of history. The story goes something like this: his mother knew John Opel who was the chairman of IBM at that time. Simultaneously, IBM was looking for software for their hardware, the newly introduced personal computer. This man promised them a software which he didn't have himself. IBM wanted to buy the software. But this guy understood the concept of securing revenue. So he told IBM, I don't want to sell the software, I will license it to you per computer. Once he understood the need of the customer, he went out to look for software and bought MS-DOS from a company called Seattle Computer Products for $75,000 and sold it to IBM and other companies on a per licence basis and made millions.

This is the story of Bill Gates and the birth of Microsoft. I don't know how he raised the $50,000 but it wouldn't be difficult to raise the capital from a deal backed by IBM. And the rest, as they say is history. They found the pain, pre-sold it, and made billions.

So, what does it take to get started as an entrepreneur? What's that one thing you need? The only thing that actually matters for you to have a business. The only thing you need is a paying customer. Just one customer to believe in you and that's it. Having a paying customer changes everything in your life.

Why is this important? For one, having a paying customer reduces your risk substantially. You don't have to guess anymore, and you'll be able to build exactly what somebody needs. This is important because you don't need a PhD, a college degree, a fancy idea or rich parents to get started.

The key takeaway here is that you need to have just one paying customer. You don't have to worry about making five thousand a month or ten thousand a month or whatever goal it is that you're focused on in the long-term. In the short-term all you want to do is just focus on getting one person to believe in you.

2. Four Criteria of Freedom

I'm going to tell you a short story about the people who made the most money in the gold rush of California. Now, the gold rush was in the early 1900s and you'd think the people who had made the most money in the gold rush were the guys digging for gold. But, as it turns out, the guys that made the most money in the gold rush were the people selling the shovels and Levi Strauss, the guy selling jeans to all the gold miners.

So, let's talk about why this is important. In Robert Kiyosaki's book Rich Dad Poor Dad, he talks about the evolution of entrepreneurship and the four phases most people go through. The first phase is where people are employees. Stuck, working for somebody else, and exchanging time for money. Generally unhappy with what they're doing.

In the second phase they become self-employed where they're running their own business, but they're still exchanging time for money. The third phase is where they become business owners, where they step out of the day-to-day operations and run the business as an entrepreneur. The fourth phase is when they become an investor wherein they invest in multiple businesses. As investors, they're above all of these different levels, just kind of looking down and operating at a really high level.

Most entrepreneurs are trapped, because they think of themselves as self-employed, but when you move to becoming a business owner that's when life opens up for you. So, let's talk about these four criteria:

First criterion: The first criterion is an automated sale. When we say automated sale, we mean that you check your bank account on Friday and there's more money in your account than there was on Monday. How does that money get there? That's the automation we're talking about.

Second criterion: No accounts receivable means you get paid upfront for your service. So you're not like a landscape designer who's going to work for 90 days and then hopes to get paid.

Third criterion: Recurring monthly revenue. That's pretty much self-explanatory.

It is difficult to acquire a customer and to get that one paying customer. To get one customer to pay a one-time fee and to get a customer to pay a monthly fee requires relatively the same amount of effort. If you're going to go through all that effort, go for the customers that are going to pay the monthly fee.

Fourth criterion: The selling tools. These are the shovels and the jeans. This means you help people achieve a certain goal.

These are the four criteria I've built my business around.

First example: My company Jetking

Automated sale: The sale happens automatically through my channels and own centres. I am not personally involved in the sales. If I was, it would have been impossible to enrol 50,000 students a year across the country.

No accounts receivable: People pay for my services first, then I give them actual service.

Recurring revenue: A typical Jetking student pays in installments where I get the monthly revenue, and in the case of a franchisee centres (my channels), I keep 30% for every rupee earned. In fact, most of my revenue comes from the top 20% of my partners.

Shovels and tools: I am not actually doing the IT services myself, but it is a tool for recruiters.

3. Entrepreneur vs Employee

You're going to learn the difference in the mind-sets of an entrepreneur and an employee.

I have always been an entrepreneur because my father was an entrepreneur.

When you make the move to become an entrepreneur, you can't look at this new world through the eyes of an employee.

Why is this important? As an entrepreneur, you're going to experience uncertainty like never before. This uncertainty will be your constant companion day in and day out. This is terrifying because it goes against everything we've been taught our entire lives since our childhood. We have always been taught that we need to know the answers and we need to know what the correct thing to do is. But when you understand the difference in the mind-set of an entrepreneur and that of an employee, you'll start to see that this uncertainty is totally normal and expected. Its okay not to know what the answers are all the time.

Here are a few things we've learnt about being an entrepreneur versus being an employee: Entrepreneurs take full responsibility for their life. Employees, they might take responsibility for their life, but they're told what to do on a daily basis. They're told when to wake up, when they're able to eat, when they're able to leave and how much money they get to make at the end of the day.

The day you wake up and realise that no one is going to take care of you and the only person who can do that is you, is a very scary day indeed. It is terrifying because you have, at that particular moment realised, you're responsible for everything in your life. You're creating everything. There is no one to blame but you. When you set out on this new path, if it weren't hard enough, every time you get rejected or told no, the terror you feel is amplified a little bit.

Remember, with positive interaction, the uncertainty only goes away for a moment, and then it comes back. So learn to make uncertainty your friend.

The next point is having the answers versus not having them. Entrepreneurs, they really sit with questions; the employee panics when an answer is not known. So, get comfortable with not knowing answers. This goes against everything we've been taught as child. We always have to know the answer; we failed in our tests if we didn't know the answers.

The sad part is that we were never taught how to ask questions.

The following story brilliantly explains the importance of asking questions:

An Insurance company was faced with a typical problem. The performance of new agents who joined the company would start declining after 18 months of their joining. This was observed for every agent who joined the organisation.

They hired a professional to do research into this issue and recommend corrective measures to be taken.

During the course of research, it was discovered that for the first eighteen months, the new agents when visiting the prospective customer asked questions like:

- How long have you lived here?
- What are your outstanding loans?
- What are the monthly installment amounts?
- What are the educational plans for your children?

After about forty-five minutes, the agent would recommend the plan that best suited the customer.

Over the period of eighteen months, the agent became an expert and with one look at the customer's house would conclude:

- The customer has lived in this house for around 5.3 years
- The loan amount is Rs. 80 lakhs
- The EMI outflow is Rs. 80,000 per month
- They have one kid

In ten minutes flat, the agent would walk in and tell the customer what financial solution was best suited for them.

The researcher concluded that the moment the agent stopped asking questions and started telling the solution, sales dropped.

The value economy versus the time economy is another point that I have learnt over the period. Entrepreneurs live in the value economy. An entrepreneur creates value once and it continues to work without him. But employees are the value themselves. When an employee stops working, the value stops, and subsequently the money also stops.

The value economy versus the time economy is really important because it is what dictates your income. Your income is directly tied to your time if you're an employee. There is no other way you are able to make money aside from exchanging time – which is a terrible way to live. Entrepreneurs, on the other hand make income that is proportionate to the value they're adding to the world. But if you try to be an entrepreneur and are focused on how much time you're putting into your business and that's the only measure, it's not going to work. You have to be focused on how much value you are adding to your customer's life.

There are instances in businesses where you could work for one hour and make five thousand or ten thousand, because you understand how to create that kind of value in one hour.

You will understand value in detail in the next chapter but for now, anything that makes your customer's life, fun, faster, easier and more profitable is adding value.

Everything is amplified when you're an entrepreneur. When you're an employee, you can just kind of go in and punch the clock, your days are relatively stable and then there are days where, you know, your boss pisses you off and you're frustrated. But when you're an entrepreneur, the highs you experience are going to be greater than any highs you've had and the lows are way more low because you will be worried about your entire business collapsing and if that happens what's going to happen to you?

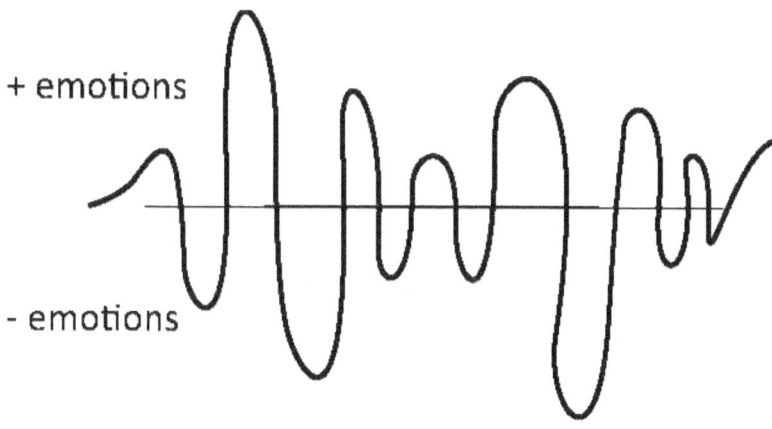

If you have been an employee your whole life, then you know, and you'd step into the entrepreneurial arena and you move from this being your experience and you think that this is actually the full experience. You're actually not aware that there are other experiences out there. You come in as an employee, you become an entrepreneur and then all of a sudden you experience your first real dose of shame and fear at such an intense level that it causes you to panic. You want to jump back to being an employee because it feels safe. Don't do that. Stay on and just realise that the entrepreneur's emotional experience is a giant pendulum.

The quality of your life is directly proportional to the level of uncertainty you can handle. If you're living life in your comfort zone, there's not a whole lot of uncertainty in it. You can live a comfortable life, but you just won't feel alive.

When I started my most successful business, Jetking, I was irrationally uncertain. It was a terrible feeling. I remember being so afraid because there were big competitors like NIIT, Aptech, etc. How was I ever going to compete with all these guys? I had massive loans, I could not sleep at night wondering how would i pay off the three crore debt, but I persevered. I stuck with the uncertainty and now it's been the most rewarding experience that I have ever had.

So, it is uncertainty versus constant stability and certainty. As an entrepreneur, you're going to face a lot more uncertainty almost daily. You don't know which government agency will come knocking asking for money. Some customer somewhere in a remote village sues you when in reality, it's his fault.

As an entrepreneur, you begin to realise that the quality of answers you get is directly proportional to the quality of questions you ask. Large number of people get hung up asking the wrong questions when they're employees. The bible says ask and you shall receive. Asking the right question is a big part of being an entrepreneur. Remember, there are no right answers but right questions.

4. Old vs New Model

We're going to talk about the old model of risky entrepreneurship versus the new model of less risky, more predictable entrepreneurship. What would it be like to build a business back in the 50s? Think about everything you would have to go through.

There are no credit cards. The only way you can accept payment is through cash or cheque, which you actually have to go to the bank and deposit. You have limited access to the people you can sell to, based on the location you're living in. You have limited access to capital or funds to get started, and it's probably going to cost a decent amount of money to get your business off the ground because you probably need some sort of a storefront.

It's frustrating because you have everything going against you. And if you did get a loan and you got all this to work, you had to figure out the product you were going to sell, which you probably had to build in a vacuum, without getting any feedback from the customers. When people say that starting a business is risky, they're right – if you were starting a business fifty years ago.

Why is this important today? It's because we're living in one of the coolest periods in history to start a business. Starting a business has never been easier. The amount of information we have at our fingertips to learn what to do is incredible. The amount of tools and resources we have online is amazing. You can start a business literally from nothing. Just get started.

It's no wonder why people think business is risky because they're thinking in the terms of '50s, but the world of entrepreneurship has completely shifted.

In the '50s it was all about guessing. Entrepreneurship was generally done by guessing and to some extent that's still true today. Today you can do the prediction instead of guessing. Guessing is where you try to imagine what your customers want. Predicting is where you give customers exactly what they want by asking them, showing them, getting feedback and iterating. This model is called the test model project. So what changes has technology brought about?

If you want to get feedback from your customers for a product that you wanted to build in the '50s for example, or even the '80s, you would either have to have a storefront, set up a little booth and talk to people one on one as they walk by, or maybe send out mailers or mail some samples, where you spend a ton of money on direct mail and then hope they respond. You then spent time sifting through all the responses. It took two or three weeks to go through all the responses and analyse them. Today, you can go on Facebook and message a bunch of people. If you have your target audience's email addresses, you can create a survey on Google Forms in thirty minutes and blast it out to receive feedback instantly.

Literally, you could have same day feedback on your product versus months, as before.

Software in the '50s was not great. You'd have to write for weeks, and then put it into a computer to test. Maybe in '80s or even the '90s you had to write software, save it on a CD and ship it out to see what customers think. When writing code today, you can make a few changes, push it out to customers and get feedback almost instantaneously.

Even writing and publishing a book used to take lakhs of rupees. It was for the few and the privileged, but today anyone can write a book or an eBook and get it published on Amazon or make their own website and sell it as an eBook.

In terms of creating a physical store front, like a brick and mortar store, if you wanted to sell t-shirts or start a furniture shop or whatever it is you found a passion for, you'd have to find a realtor, find a location, rent a space, redesign, renovate, redecorate, go to the bank, get a Rs. 10,00,000 loan, spend eight weeks getting a whole store ready and then hope that customers come. Today, in ten minutes, you can set up an e-commerce store with Shopify.com and be up and running.

If you wanted to build an e-commerce store in the '90s, just fifteen years ago, it would cost you tens of thousands of rupees just to get the website set up. Now, with Shopify the investment is just Rs. 1000 a month.

You can sell anything at a fraction of the cost. Today, with sites like Quikr and OLX, you can sell anything at a higher price to the user who needs it directly thereby eliminating the middle man and all the inefficiencies.

People are communicating through WhatsApp rather than SMS. Transactions worth millions of rupees happen on technology platforms such as WhatsApp and the amount is increasing, each day.

The reason I am sharing this is because there has never been a bigger opportunity for you to create wealth for yourself and your family. There is an abundance of resources all around us, and it is because technology has facilitated it. We have so many opportunities now unlike anything we've ever seen before.

A number of people tell me it's harder to make money in today's market because of the competition, but if you take a look at Henry Ford or Bill Gates, these guys built their billion dollar empire in ten or twenty years and Facebook became a billion dollar company in a matter of five years or less. And the next billionaire will be created even faster than *Zuckerberg*. So, the amount of wealth accumulation is speeding up because of technology.

With that in mind, let's jump into some examples of businesses that have been created following this trend so you can see for yourself.

WhatsApp was bought by Facebook for $19 billion (approx. Rs. 120000 crores). The company which developed this app, is just a few years old. What's fascinating is that WhatsApp had only thirty-four employees.

At the time of writing this book, Flipkart had raised over $3.15 billion (approx. Rs 17000 crores) and this is just the tip of the iceberg.

5. Blue Glasses

The Blue Glasses: seeing abundance everywhere.

There is a famous story spoken in management circles. It's a story of how Bata, the shoe company, entered India. The head of market research for Bata was sent to India to see if there was a market for shoes in India, because at that point Indians just wore Indian slippers. Simultaneously, another shoe company sent their research head to do a similar study. After three months of study, the other company executive went back and reported there was no market for shoes since no one wore shoes. The market research head of Bata went to the board and reported that there was a huge market since no one wore shoes in India. Finding opportunities and problems to solve everywhere is one of the keys to becoming a successful entrepreneur.

Why is this important? As you can tell by the stories, the perspective in which you see the world can change everything. The Blue Glasses is a perspective to view abundance, opportunity and pains to be solved everywhere you're looking. You can constantly choose to put these glasses on at first, and then after a while seeing the world this way becomes second nature. The question that's constantly running in the back of our minds is how we can make life easier, faster, fun and more profitable. How can we add more value to people's lives?

How do you feel when you ask that question? There's like an expansive, excitement to life.

Let's take an everyday example about how to wear Blue Glasses. As you get up, do you think there is a pain you are going through that you want to solve?

Will there be other people who want to solve this pain? Maybe it's the bed or the pillow you're sleeping on. Then you go to your washroom. Is there some level of discomfort you have that you think other people might be having which they are willing to pay to solve? On your way to the office, you are standing at a bus stand and people are standing with you. You ask them about their life and what pain they might be experiencing. And then there might be one guy who says he wants admission for his son in a certain school. If you can help him out, you do. If you can't, you might know someone who could. And maybe if 100 people have the same problem, you can start a business around it. These are just examples of wearing a blue glass till this habit becomes second nature. As long as you have this skill, you can never be poor.

This is not typically how you go about with a disruptive idea selection. This is me looking at the world, recognising pain and saying, "You know what? That seems inefficient. That seems painful. How can I solve it? How can we make the current solution faster, fun, easier, and more profitable?"

When you're on your disruptive idea selection, people are going to be talking about pain all the time. As you hear these painful things, there are questions running in your mind such as, "How can I make this faster, fun, easier and profitable?"

You're probably not going to have the 100 crore idea or the idea for your product based on this first initial thought, but it's a step down the rabbit hole (from Alice in Wonderland which takes Alice to a whole new and wonderful world) and it's just to get you moving. You're just looking at the world and seeing all these different opportunities and then the one idea that you have is probably going to pivot and lead to something else that might lead to something else. But what are the areas where you can just get started and get moving?

I recently read about a company that was valued at approx. 18.2 billion dollars (approx. 1 lakh crore). It is called Uber, which launched a mobile app where people could book a taxi service with a click of a button.

Here is the brief on Wikipedia for Uber:

Uber is a venture-funded start-up and transportation network company based in San Francisco, California, that makes mobile apps connecting passengers with drivers of vehicles for hire and ridesharing services. The company arranges pickups in dozens of cities around the world. Cars are reserved by using a mobile app (which can also be used by customers to track their reserved car's location).

Initially, Uber drivers used cars such as Lincoln Town, Cadillac Escalades, BMW 7 Series, and Mercedes-Benz S550 sedans. After 2012, Uber launched UberX, following the addition of a wider selection of cars to appeal to a broader cross-section of the market. In 2012, Uber announced a plan to expand its operations to include ridesharing in non-taxi vehicles.

In June 2014, Uber completed a round of funding, valuing the company at US$18.2 billion. Although Uber has not released the names of its investors, Fidelity Investments has been widely reported to lead the investment. As of August 2014, the company continues to deal with accusations in several jurisdictions of illegal taxicab operations.

6. Goal Setting on Steroids

What is your goal?

According to Wikipedia a goal is a desired result or possible outcome that a person or a system envisions, plans and commits to achieve a personal or organisational desired endpoint in some sort of assumed development. Many people endeavour to reach goals within a finite time by setting a deadline.

It is extremely important for people who want to become entrepreneurs, to decide how much

money they want to make. In the bible it says without vision people perish. If you do not have a goal you will be lost. Even if you are reaching success you wouldn't know if you are heading in the right direction. "If you don't know where to go any road will take you there" - Alice in Wonderland

Every human being has RAS (Reticular activation system) What is reticular activating system?

This system is considered the brain's attention centre. It is the key for switching on your brain and also considered as the main centre of motivation.

The reticular activating system is connected to the spinal cord at its base from where it accepts information which comes from the ascending sensory tracts directly. It travels up to the mid brain and while going up forms a complex neuron collection that acts as convergence point for signals from the interior environment as well as the external surroundings. So, Reticular activating system is a place where your thoughts, internal feelings and the outside influences converge. It is very skilled in producing dynamic effects on the motor activity centres located in the brain and the cortex activity such as the frontal lobes.

When you set a goal your RAS gets activated. So when your RAS gets activated your whole body goes in one direction in achieving your goal, when you have not set a goal your RAS is dispersed all over and your chances of achieving your goal drastically reduces. Let's set some goals right now.

So imagine this: someone gives you a 500-piece jigsaw puzzle. You are so enthusiastic about putting the pieces together, and you look for the reference picture on the lid of the box, there's nothing there. It's blank. So now how will you know which piece goes where if you don't know what the final picture is? Now apply this example to your own life.

That picture on the lid of the puzzle box is your goal, it is the BIG PICTURE. The 500 pieces are your talents, learning, experience, family, friends, etc. In order to complete the puzzle, you have to join the pieces together so they fit and therefore, complete the 'BIG PICTURE', then you will be aimlessly wasting your time and effort trying to make various pieces fit to create a non-existent picture.

In life, know what the BIG PICTURE is before you start. In other words, know what your goal is. The key is in knowing what you want. The unconscious mind is constantly processing information and in turn we automatically move in that direction. If you don't know where to go, any road will take you there.

Maxwell Maltz call this 'psycho-cybernetics' in his well known book of the same title. When the mind has a defined target, it can focus and direct and refocus and redirect until it reaches its intended goal. In this chapter you will

learn how to formulate your goals and dreams and desires, how to fix firmly in your mind what you want and how to get it.

7. Winning starts with beginning

Once you define your goal, working towards it will become easier. Defining your goals is simply creating a map of your life. What is your destination, and how you would like to get there?

Take the example of a word-class batsman. If he were blindfolded, how many ball? Setting a goal is simply taking the blindfold off. Once the batsman sees that ball is coming, he can very well hit a *sixer!*

There are three kinds of goals we have short-term, middle term and long-term.

All these are time –bound but you must have them. Just consider this: At age 20, 40 seems far away - and age 60 seems unthinkable. But when you reach age 40, you wonder what you did between 20 and 40 years and then again, at age 60, most adults look back sadly and wonder how they wasted their precious time without achieving anything at all. They wished they could do it all over again.

But in real life, there is no replay. That's why, to get on this world, you need to get a life RIGHT NOW!

The Power of Focus

Your short-term and middle term goals must help you achieve your long-term goals. If they don't, perhaps what is missing in your life is focus. Which is exactly why goal setting works.

Before we talk about our goal setting, here are some examples of focus.

1. Engineers have determined that the pressure, per square inch, is actually greater from the average woman's single high heel shoe than from an elephant's foot. I know this may sound strange but this is because all the woman's weight and power is focused in that tiny heel, whereas an elephant's weight and power is spread over a larger, broader area.
2. Remember the little experiment you did in your early school days? Focusing the sun's rays through a magnifying glass and starting a fire?

Sunrays do not normally start fires by themselves because the heat is diffused over a large area i.e. the atmosphere. But, focus those rays on a small surface and you will start a fire.

The lesson to be learnt from these examples is that when you direct all your weight, energy, creativity, power and effort on achieving a very specific goal, you benefit from the power of focus.

So let's say you want to reach a point where you are earning Rs. 5,00,000 a month. So take out a blank piece of paper and draw a picture of yourself on the left side of the paper and draw Rs. 5,00,000 a month goal on the right side of the paper. Here is what I want you to do. Make a list of all the activities you do in the day in the left column. Every time you move forward toward your goals, I want you to make an arrow pointing toward your goal, which means you have moved one step forward toward your goal.

Now, I want you to list everything you do in the whole day. So let's take an example of *Rahul* and his typical day.

- He opens his eyes, goes to the washroom, brushes his teeth and has tea. So he cannot make an arrow since this doesn't move him forward toward his goal.
- Then he opens his Facebook account and checks his email. This doesn't move him forward toward his goal either.
- Before long, it's so obvious that he doesn't do anything to move toward the goal.

On the other hand, let's take an example of *Rohit*, who has a different routine.

He gets up at 5 a.m., does his meditation, works out and schedules items for the day.

6 a.m.: He does his most important activity of the day, which is to make a presentation for an MNC firm or product creation.

After that he has a nourishing breakfast and starts the most important activity in any business: meeting new clients for two hours and existing clients for another two hours.

Breakfast is the most important meal of the day. A good breakfast provides the brain with fuel after an overnight fast. Without a good breakfast you are running on an empty stomach and trying to do an important activity at this time is like starting a car without petrol.

By 12, he has finished the important activities of the day. The most important activity is always understanding your customers and getting in touch with them. So, it's not that we don't go on Facebook or check emails. We want to do the most important, revenue generation activities early in the day, and the rest of the activities can be done later.

Some people spend almost half a day answering emails and at the end of the day they think they are working hard, but they are also upset that no money is coming in.

In the space provided below, draw a picture of yourself in the left column. In the right column, write your goals. In the left column, write the activities you do during the course of the day. For the activity that takes you closer towards the goal, draw an arrow from the left column to the right column.

Draw a picture of yourself	Your Goals
Write a list of activities you do in a day	

Each morning you must ask the question, "What is the highest leverage activity that I should do today that will take me forward to my goal of Rs. 5,00,000 a month?" At different stages it's a different priority. In the beginning, it's just understanding the customers and getting in touch with them.

Once you have a certain set of customers, operations and services, the last level is scaling, like a franchise model or turning it into an app.

But at each level, understanding the customer and getting in touch with them is the highest leverage activity.

8. Speed of Daily Disciplined Action

In one of the classic books, Good to Great by Jim Collins, there's a story of two teams going to the North Pole. Both of them are travelling to the North Pole. One group's philosophy is to travel on the good weather days and to travel as far as they can. Another team's philosophy is to travel 20 miles each day, regardless of the weather. Even if they could actually go more, they stopped and travelled no more than 20 miles every day to conserve their energy.

If you fast forward to the end, the group that went only on the good weather days ended up dying and they didn't even make it. On the other hand, the group travelling not more than 20 miles every day not only made it, but they made it there and back on time. They came back alive and successful.

What was the difference between the two groups? Well, one group made consistent action every day and another group just kind of inconsistently worked in short bursts. I find that most people that do the 20-mile march daily, almost achieve success as compared to those who don't. Not only that, they are happier, more productive and they are more consistent in the long-term.

Have you heard about the classic story of Rabbit and the Tortoise - from Aesop's fable? It teaches us an important lesson: People who cross the finishing line are those who make daily incremental progress over a time, not the ones who take inconsistent blocks of action and burn out or crash.

I am not saying you have to work eight hours a day. You just need to work three hours. Pick the highest leverage activity and do that first.

Now, what do you mean by speed of daily disciplined action? There was a research done wherein they studied successful people. One of the main skills that they discovered was that successful people displayed their ability to execute an idea. Speed of execution refers to the speed at which one executes an idea. The point from which one decides to implement an idea to the point he actually executes it must be quick, and the person who does this the fastest will be the most successful. If you have any thought of success in life, you will start to realise that it was because you were consistently taking disciplined actions achieve that goal, whether it is losing weight, making money, getting into a relationship or learning a skill.

The information I have given here is gold only when you are consistently taking action on it. In *Sindhi*, there is a saying that one day without business takes you five days backwards. Hundreds of thousands of people will read this book, but few people will become successful. What's the difference between all people who will become successful versus failures? Successful people will take actions daily.

When I started hardware and networking institute, I learnt about a great trainer, Bob Pike who owned a company called Creative Training Techniques in Minneapolis, Minnesota, USA. I had gone with my family for vacation to the USA. My brother told me about this training programme and insisted that I attend. So I sent my wife and kids back since my kids' schools were reopening. I attended the training programme by Creative Training Techniques on how to make training fun, faster and easier.

After I returned, I read five chapters. I created slides, brochures and created the Indian version of the course content, I practised daily. It was scary in the beginning but with daily practice, managed to overcome my fears. Finally, I presented in front of my managers and friends. A not so complimentary feedback from one of the participants shattered my confidence. Not the one to lose hope, I persisted and scheduled another programme after sixty days which was a success.

Those two days were life changing for me since it had solutions to all the problems I was facing in managing a training institute. I used the workbook given in the training programme as a bible to grow my business for the next two years. I kept referring to the workbook whenever I faced any problems. Just attending the training programme wouldn't have been that helpful. I took daily disciplined action to achieve the results. Many people attended that programme, but few people actually became successful.

The truth is that we are in the information Age, but information alone is not enough. If all we needed were ideas and positive thinking, then we all would have had ponies when we were kids and we would all be living our 'dream life' now.

Action is what unites every type and form of success. Action is what produces results. Knowledge is only potential power until it comes into the hands of someone who knows how to get himself to take effective action.

This book is about taking the kind of daily disciplined action that leads to overwhelming results. If I were to say to you in two words what this book is about, they would be, "Producing Results!"

To summarise, "information is power only when it is acted upon daily and in a disciplined manner."

9. Just Say Yes

What we've noticed is that this is one of the common traits amongst the most successful entrepreneurs. They're always saying yes and they worry about

how to get things done later. When you say yes, it gives you a constraint to work against. There's a deadline; there's an order that needs to be fulfilled. Your mind is forced to come up with answers because there is a hard constraint that it has to work against. All of the top entrepreneurs, including Bill Gates, said yes before even knowing how they were actually going to the build the product they promised.

So, the problem with saying yes is that it's scary and that's why most people think "Well, I'm not sure if I can do that so I'm not going to try." However, by doing that you rob yourself of the opportunity to grow and push. Say yes and figure it out. The more often you say yes the more opportunities are going to come your way.

It is a bit easier to say yes when you have a coach or mentor or a team of entrepreneurs you are exchanging ideas with.

Now, two caveats: Saying yes causes you to move super-fast. You will be cruising at super speeds. Because you'll be cruising so fast, it will cause you to make more mistakes. This is just a natural by-product of moving quickly. So, remember that it's okay.

Second caveat once you say 'Yes', you may start taking things for granted and take little action after that, that's the danger zone.

10. Reverse Engineering: How to Get Paid Even Before You Start a Business

I will now tell you how to pre-sell a service or a product and get paid upfront even before you actually execute the product. In order to do that, you have to understand the difference between starting a business with the focus on the product and starting a business with the focus on pain.

When you start a business focused on a product, there's no guesswork involved. There is, however, a lot of anxiety in the process and an enormous amount of risk. It's the traditional way most people think about starting a business.

This is what we call "Starting a Business Forward" and is much slower than actually flipping it and starting a business backwards. When you start reverse engineering, there's little risk. It's faster and it's not traditional. It's really counter-intuitive. All the businesses I've started traditionally forward have failed and those that I've reverse engineered succeeded. The reason being when you reverse engineer, you start with a customer.

I want you to understand that when you're starting a business, flip it from thinking about the product first to thinking about the customer first and talking to them about pain.

If I can help you picture anything right now, I would say that the traditional path to building a business is like a string. What I see most entrepreneurs do with the traditional path is take the string and try to push it. The string gets all bundled up and if they keep pushing harder and harder, then it gets entangled. There's nothing you can do with the string.

Well, there's another way of starting with pain. It's actually like letting the string pull you with the customer. You are just letting them pull you. In order to let them pull you, you've got to let go of everything you're holding on to, whether it's the product idea you have, the product name or whatever it is that you're trying to hold on to. Just let go and let the customer pull you through.

The way to do that is to ask a lot of questions to really understand your customer's needs. Questions like:

1. What are your goals for the next 3–5 years?
2. What are the challenges you are facing in achieving those goals?
3. What is your top priority in your life right now?
4. What are the challenges you are facing to achieve your top priority?
5. Tell me about your typical day.
6. What are a few challenges you are facing in your day that you would like to outsource, delegate, or hire someone else to do?
7. What's the cost of your current challenge?
8. How much are you willing to pay to solve this problem?
9. What will happen if you don't solve this problem?
10. What will happen if you do solve this problem?

You cannot just ask these questions like *Paresh Rawal* of *Judaai* (who kept on asking irrelevant questions). When you are asking these questions you have to notice and write down the pain points described by your customer. Repeat the words that the customer uses back to him to establish trust and connection.

The following example illustrates the case of a person who wants to start a training business:

1. What are your goals for the next 3–5 years?
   Establish a training company of my own.
2. What are the challenges you are facing in achieving those goals?
   Lead generation – generate 100 qualified leads.
   Marketing activities
3. What Is Your Top Priority In Your Life Right Now?
   Reach out to organisations that are looking for trainers to develop their teams.

4. What are the challenges you are facing to achieve your top priority?

   Not able to generate sufficient leads.

5. Tell me about your typical day.

   Getup at 5 a.m.

   Exercise

   Have breakfast

   Visit clients and do the follow up of training programmes conducted. Review the progress of the participants.

   Create content for upcoming training programmes.

6. What are a few challenges you are facing in your day that you would like to outsource, delegate, or hire someone else to do?

   Lead generation.

7. What's the cost of your current challenge?

   Rs. 2,00,000 in lost contracts.

8. How much are you willing to pay to solve this problem?

   Rs. 20,000 per month.

9. What will happen if you don't solve this problem?

   I will not be able to meet my financial goals.

10. What will happen if you do solve this problem?

    I will be able to start my organisation sooner.

In the space provided below, speak with a potential customer or your friend and identify his or her needs:

11. What are your goals for the next 3–5 years?

    _____
    _____
    _____

12. What are the challenges you are facing in achieving those goals?

    _____
    _____
    _____

13. What is your top priority in your life right now?
_____
_____
_____
_____

14. What are the challenges you are facing to achieve your top priority?
_____
_____
_____
_____

15. Tell me about your typical day.
_____
_____
_____
_____

16. What are a few challenges you are facing in your day that you would like to outsource, delegate, or hire someone else to do?
_____
_____
_____
_____

17. What's the cost of your current challenge?
_____
_____
_____
_____

18. How much are you willing to pay to solve this problem?
_____
_____
_____
_____

19. What will happen if you don't solve this problem?

_____
_____
_____
_____

20. What will happen if you do solve this problem?

_____
_____
_____
_____

Listen intently: When you are asking these questions, the key is to listen with 100% mindfulness. You must be completely aware of the person in front of you as well as what he/she is saying. Put your phone on silent and log off from Facebook and WhatsApp. You need to be 100% committed so as to really understand the customer's problem. It's fine if you don't understand at first, dig deeper. If there is anything you don't understand, ask them more questions.

One of the techniques that has been used to its fullest is to communicate that you are listening. Say words like 'uh huh', 'yes'. Nod your head. Person should see that you are listening.

I will get into the theory behind why you ask these questions in the subsequent chapters, but these questions are a gold mine to get paid even before you start any business. These questions are your pathway to freedom.

11. Self-Analysis: Overcome Any Obstacle

"If you keep on doing things that you always have been doing, you will get the results that you have been getting."

Govinda, a movie star, in one of his interviews explained how he became so good. The way he did it was that he watched his movies forty times and asked himself how he could have done it better the next time. He kept doing

that for months until his comic timing was so tight that he became a sensation across the world.

A self-analysis will give you insights into how you can improve the next day.

At the end of every training programme, I give all my participants a sheet in which they have to fill out three things:

1. Start: Based on what they learnt today, what will they start doing today that they didn't do before?
2. Stop: Based on what they learnt today, what will they stop doing they used to do before?
3. Continue: Based on what they learnt today, what will they continue doing that they did well?

Similarly, I do that with myself regularly, which gives me lot of insight on how to change my behaviour.

Self-analysis may be one of the most sobering, revealing, uncomfortable, empowering experiences you will ever do. It allows you to see all of the unconscious habits sabotaging you. So, self-analysis allows you to become aware of undesirable behaviour and brings about a shift so you can get what you want. Once you apply awareness and consciousness to a habit, it begins to shift. If you don't self-analyse, you'll continue to use the same sabotaging behaviour you have now and this will severely slow and impede your progress. Try self-reflection once with the questions given here and see how you feel afterwards, because reflection is power.

When reflecting on a disruptive idea selection, you can ask questions such as:

- What went well about that call? Not only the content or information, but what did I do really well?
- What went bad about that call? How did I fail or how did I not execute and do what I wanted to do best?
- If there's one thing I did in this call I wish I wouldn't do on the next call, what's that?
- What's the one thing I did hear that I want to stop?
- What do I know now that I didn't know before? Chances are I learnt something. So this makes me feel positive even if I fared poorly on the call.

12. Training: How to Amplify Learning and Retention Forever TRAIN:

Train yourself, your partners, and customers all the time "There is nothing that training cannot do. Nothing is above its reach or below it. It can turn bad morals to good, good morals to bad; it can destroy principles, it can recreate them; it can debase angels to men and lift men to angelship." - Mark Twain

I have been fortunate enough to understand early on in my life that training is extremely important. I don't know how I got it. Maybe it was my father, who made me realise the importance of training. If you have heard the saying, "Put your money where your mouth is," here it is. I have spent more money on training my staff, franchisees, and students than anything else.

My first encounter with training was making the booklet for do-it-yourself radio kits. I also taught electronics as a teacher at *Kamla* High School.

When I lost my business and was contemplating on what to do next, training was the first and last thing that came to my mind. My father-in law mocked me many times, saying "What is this training institute that you have started? There is no profit from this." Manufacturing was big back then. People looking at me and what I was doing thought I was weird to get into training. But I knew the value of training and how it had changed my life.

What is the definition of training?

According to Google, the definition of training is as follows:

Training

1. *The Action of Teaching a Person or Animal a Particular Skill or Type of Behaviour.*

According to Wikipedia

Training is the acquisition of knowledge, skills, and competencies as a result of the teaching of vocational or practical skills and knowledge that relate to specific useful competencies. Training has specific

goals of improving one's capability, capacity, productivity and performance. It forms the core of apprenticeships and provides the backbone of content at institutes of technology (also known as technical colleges or polytechnics). In addition to the basic training required for a trade, occupation or profession, observers of the labour-market recognise as of 2008, the need to continue training beyond initial qualifications: to maintain, upgrade and update skills throughout working life. People within many professions and occupations may refer to this sort of training as professional development.

Why do you need to train?

I want you to think of the biggest problem you are facing right now. If you want to solve it, you need to be trained. Either you get trained or learn from a book, video or training programme. You take help from a coach or consultant. Your wealth is directly proportional to the training you have in that particular field.

If you get stuck somewhere, it is important to ask what you need to learn today to get unstuck.

When I got my business model correct, I realised the only way to grow my business was continuous training: training myself, employees, business partners, etc. *Noel Tichy* of GE calls this the virtuous teaching cycle and this is the only way to develop leaders.

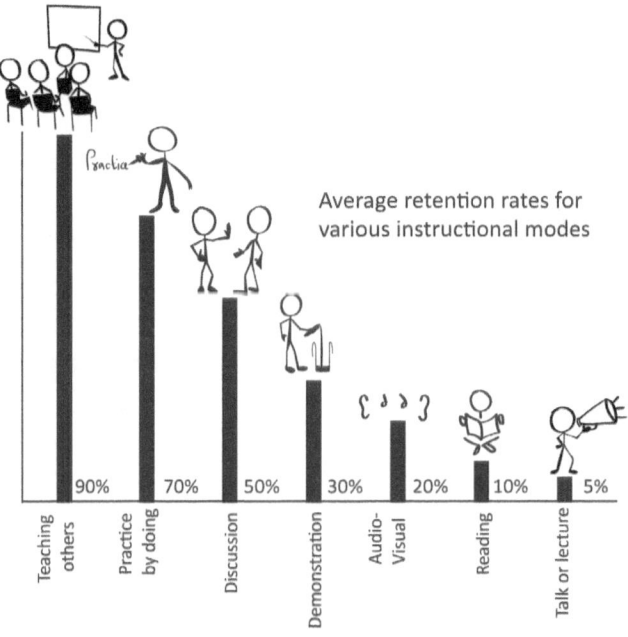

I had created a proprietary training programme called Smartrain. This was for managers on how to be a leader. One of the core components of this programme was how to make training fun, faster and easier.

Every employee undergoes this training programme in Jetking. I used to wonder what the best way was for them to retain this knowledge. I was aware of the research which stated that you remember about 10% of what you read, 20% of what you see or hear, 30% of what you see as a demonstration or example, 50% of what you discuss in a group, 75% of what you practice and 90% of what you teach.

Once they attend the training programme, at the end of the session they have to give a presentation of what they have learnt. Just by giving a presentation, they enhanced their learning and retention by 90%.

Even in our classes, three students are asked to come in front of the class and present what they learnt the day before.

To train someone, you have to read each word carefully, make notes and put it in PowerPoint slide as bullet points, and when you teach someone, that learning goes into your subconscious mind.

Every year my franchisees are given a book. They have to read the book, make a presentation and come train other business partners. I clearly remember the year where they had to make a presentation on Stephen Covey's 8th Habit.

By the end of the whole session there was such a charge amongst the business partners and employees. Not only did we grow that year, but I could see a marked difference in their value system. So if you want to master this book or anything for that matter, the best approach is to teach it to others.

At the age of sixteen, my eldest son got mixed up with some bad friends and started smoking and drinking. I wanted him to quit and develop some good habits. So I gave him a small book on success and told him that if he goes to each class and trains students on this topic of success, I will give him Rs. 50 per session. In those days Rs. 50 was a big amount and he always wanted to buy a mobile phone, which was just introduced in India. He used to train students for almost 4–6 hours on success. Now he doesn't smoke or drink, and he is one of the most prolific trainers in the country.

I personally feel, India as a country doesn't value training as much as people in other countries. Most of the Jetking faculties actually want to work in the industry. As a fresher, they don't get easy entry in the industry, so they join Jetking and by the end of two years, they are so strong they get big hikes in salary - double and sometimes triple the salary at Jetking.

One of the key successes of Jetking is organising biannual training conferences where all business partners assemble at a place and leave their egos outside. They learn about the success and failures of the previous year and what were the best practices of successful business partners. These are typically three to four-day training sessions where on the first day or the second day there are external trainers who train them on various topics like motivation, sales, hiring, maintaining quality, etc.

Successful business partners share their best practices so others can learn. When they train on what they did successfully, it gives them a different level of confidence because other business partners are looking up to them.

I hear a lot of people tell me that making faculties or business partners meet is not a good idea, they might gang up against us. Many a times, our business partners don't want to send their faculty or employees for training programmes because they feel they will become too powerful and leave the job. I have experienced that if you train people, they are subconsciously indebted to you. They start considering you as a platform for growth and the retention is higher. Yes, some people might leave or some people might gang up against you, but that's a good thing because they were not the kind of the people right for the job in the first place. Now you know who's here to grow and who is here for passing time.

I have realised that lot of learning happens when the business partners talk to each other during lunches, at dinner tables or during drinks where they get a little comfortable sharing their actual strategies.

The Ebbinghaus curve of forgetting states that if you learn a concept once in 30 days you will retain just 10% of the content, but if you learn a concept six times through various methods, you will remember 90% of the content. Each student goes through a theory session, practical exams, group discussions, presentations, quizzes, and tests in order to remember the lesson. Hence the majority of students, who complete the Jetking course, are placed in good companies with a good salary even though they might not have a good academic background.

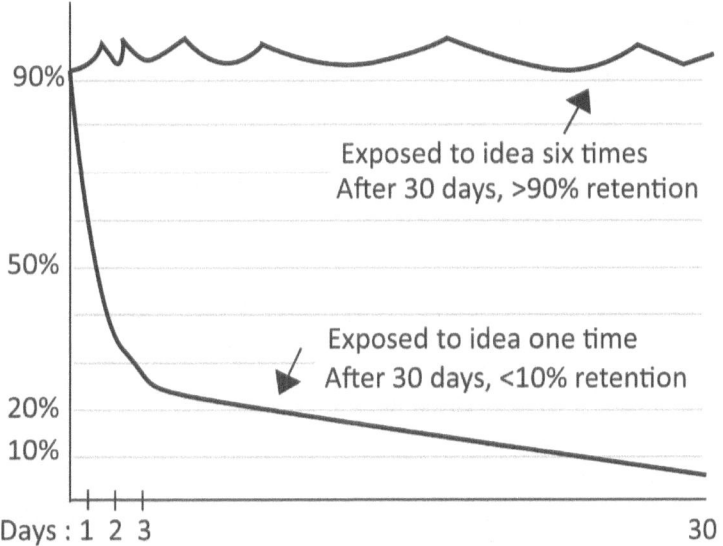

In any training matrix there are five levels of competencies. For you to master any skill, you have to go through these levels.

Five Levels of Competencies

(*Five Levels of Competence adapted from William Howell*)

Level 1: Unconscious Incompetence – When I first sat in the driver's seat to drive a car, I believed that I could drive it. I was not competent, but I didn't know it. In an instant, I moved to level 2.

Level 2: Conscious Incompetence – First time I turned key in the ignition and put the car into drive mode, it jumped and stalled. It was at this moment I realised, that I was incompetent.

Level 3: Conscious Competence - After lot of practice, I could drive the car, but I was always tense about my abilities. It was difficult to relax.

Level 4: Unconscious Competence - I no longer had to think about everything that driving a car involved because the act had become automatic.

Level 5: Conscious Unconscious Competence - Not only I am competent and can run on autopilot, but I can verbalise to others how I am able to do what I do.

Now I can teach other people how to drive.

You're going to learn about the five levels of learning and the cycle we all go through to learn anything. It doesn't matter if you're learning copywriting or learning to play the piano or learning to play tennis. This is the same process and the same framework that we all go through regardless of what it is that we're learning.

When you understand the process and the framework, it will add comfort to the journey because you won't feel as stressed. You'll know exactly where you're at in the process and you know exactly where you're going next.

Stage One: Unconscious incompetence. This is where we all start. If you imagine yourself trying to learn the piano for the first time, there's this sense of wonder, awe and excitement and this joyful anticipation of what you're about to learn. The reason you feel that is because you  don't know what you don't know yet. It's a whole new world. That's why this phase is generally pretty fun.

Stage Two: This is when it gets a little bit harder. Conscious incompetence is stage two. This is where you have that holy crap moment where you realise there's a big world that exists and you had no idea that it was there. So, when you look at learning how to start a profitable business in six months, it's like wow! There is so much stuff to learn and so much stuff to do and you have this moment where you realise you have no idea what you're doing with this and you don't really know where to go next.

This part can be stressful and a little painful. The good thing to know is that when you start feeling stressed, feeling overwhelmed and a little bit of pain, it's a good sign. That's just life telling you that you're moving on to the next phase, the phase of conscious competence.

How long does this phase last? It totally depends on you. The quality of your experience is directly proportional to the uncertainty you are ready to deal with.

Some people might take more time while some people might take less. If you are conversant with, let's say, selling skills, communication skills or listening skills, it might be faster for you versus someone who is into software coding but has no idea on how to listen properly or do a sales call. It's kind of like riding a bike. You don't ride a bike a million miles an hour in your first try, but you catch on really, really fast. So, it's a skill like riding a bike. Daily disciplined and focused actions speeds up this phase. It's how intensely you're doing it, how consistent you are and how much you reflect on it. To get my first students or franchisee, it took a very long time. The second took less time. The third took even less. Today it's automatic.

Stage Three: This is where things begin to be a bit more fun. At this point you realise you know the basics of what you're doing. You've been doing it for a while, you've been conscious, focused and aware of the effort you're putting in. You get to the point where you become conscious of your conscious competence.

Just think about riding a bike. If you try it once a week for three months or if you try it every day for ten days, you're going to learn how to ride it in a much different way.

That intensity of focus and total absorption and immersion is important. However, as much as you immerse yourself in step two is how quickly you'll come out at step three. It's not a matter of talent; it's a matter of something you can actually control. As you continue doing it throughout step three, eventually you'll end up at stage four.

Stage Four: Unconscious competence. This is exciting because you become a master at some level of whatever it is that you're learning. You may not be a master wherein you're the best in the world but a master none the less, where you can do it without even thinking about it. It's just a part of you and your personality.

Stage Five: Conscious unconscious competence. This is what I am trying to do in this book and really understand how I did what I did and how I can teach this to others. If you can develop a system around what you have mastered, therein lies the real value.

This is why many billionaires or multi-millionaires aren't really that good at teaching you how to make money because it's an unconscious competence for them. That's why a lot of Olympians who are the best can't really teach you the process they followed to master their sport.

13. Superstars

We're going to talk about the difference between superstars and everyone else.

Let's dive into some of the distinctions between the superstars and then everyone else.

Both people who are superstars and those who are not start off a little excited and a little nervous.

The first difference between a superstar and an average person is the "Why." The superstars, the second step of the high achievers, create a reason why. If you create a strong why, that is a massive leverage you have created. One of the biggest reasons why I created the world's largest IT training institute was to get rid of the massive debt I had accumulated. If I didn't have the pressure to get rid of my debt, I probably wouldn't have reached this level. You know, as they say, necessity is the mother of invention. I am not saying go out there and take a massive loan, but having a strong why will give you a drive like you never had before.

A few whys can be:

1. To make my parents proud
2. To buy a house in five years
3. To buy a sports car
4. To get the girl of my life

I don't know what your why will be, but it has to be emotionally exciting and motivating for you.

> "Give me a lever long enough and a fulcrum on which to place it and I'll move the world
>
> —*Archimedes*

The why is your lever.

1. *Why do you want to start a business?*
2. *Superstars view the results as learning in progress* and everybody else views the results as either a success or failure. If it's a failure, they beat themselves up over it really hard.
3. *If super stars get stuck, they reach out for help* whereas everybody else feels helpless and are under the impression that they are bothering people if they reach out. Whenever I get stuck in a business problem I immediately call *Vijay Sampat*, Ex-CEO of *Amar Chitra Katha* and seek his guidance. Sometimes I also call *John Cherian*, another old friend of mine. Based on the problem, I try to think who is an expert at solving this particular problem and get in touch with him. I don't stop there, either. I speaks to my sons, my manager or my brother, and after that, based on my hunch and intuition, I make my decision. Two things happen when you speak about your problems to someone else. One, you verbalise and put it out there. Things are very different when they are in your head versus when you speak it out to someone. The act of speaking out your problem itself decreases the intensity of the problem and you are more emotionally unbiased towards the problem. You will come away with a better solution. Secondly, you get a third person's perspective.
4. *Superstars repeat like there is no tomorrow.* Repetition is the mother of skills. When I launched my training programme Smartrain, I was not a confident speaker. I hired a guy named Lobo to coach me to be a confident speaker. He asked me to fold my hands and repeat a paragraph at least a 100 times. For the past twenty-five years in Jetking, I have kept repeating the mission

of my company, the same strategy. If you keep repeating it, you will make those words second nature. Superstars, rinse and repeat this behaviour to achieve rapid results.

5. *Superstars view problems as solvable.* Struggling people view problems as bad. So, you know a superstar when they've encountered a problem and they're like, "Yeah, I've got this problem and I'm really trying to figure it out." And then you've got everybody else and they're like, "Oh, yeah, I've got this problem and I just don't know what to do."

6. That's kind of the language you might hear them use. There is a saying that problems are the breakfast of champions. Superstars love problems, and understand the problems better. Who are the people who don't have problems? "Dead people." A lot of people tell me their goal is to not have any problems. I tell them that if they reach that place, they will be dead. The minute you have a problem, get excited, celebrate that you are alive. The minute you solve that problem, you will grow to the next level. The more problems you solve, the more you will grow. There is also kind of a person that I call "not in touch with reality." They have all sorts of problems, but they can't even see them. They are conditioned by movies and TV series to such an extent they can't differentiate between an illusion and reality.

7. *Superstars create results.* Average people create excuses. When you talk to high achievers, all you will ever hear about are the results they're making, whereas everybody else will create excuses. I ask people about their goals and then I ask them if they have achieved them. Many tell me they have not achieved them. I ask them why. Here are some of the excuses they come up with.

    1. Government is bad
    2. My family is not rich
    3. It's too hot in my city (I was surprised to hear this)
    4. If I was in the USA, I would have succeeded
    5. I don't know the right people
    6. I am not educated enough

    And many more such excuses. If you study successful people and their background, all of them have achieved results despite any excuses you can think of. People like *Dhirubhai Ambani, Mark Zuckerberg, Laxmi Mittal, Bharti Mittal, Milkha Singh*, etc.

8. *Superstars get in with 100% commitment.* As you must have heard, the saying of the *Salman Khan*: "Once I commit, I don't even listen to myself."

When I started the Jetking School of Electronic Technology, I had no option. I was either going to die or succeed. I have handled over one hundred franchisees over the years and one of the key success criteria is that they give their 100% and not do anything else. Franchisees that have many businesses have a very low chance of success. You need to be 100% committed to one thing in order to achieve success.

For the past twenty-five years, my focus has been just on Jetking and one course, JCHNP (Jetking Certified Hardware and Networking Professional). I have refined it like a diamond and reaped my rewards. *Warren Buffet* researches for the whole year and finally invests in one stock. But he commits 100% to it. I reject hundreds of franchisees every year because they cannot commit only to Jetking. Even when you're looking to start a business, you cannot be 95% committed, nor 96%, 97%, 98%, not even 99% committed. It has to be 100%. I hear a lot of people starting a business along with three other businesses they have. They don't commit 100% to it, the business fails and they say it didn't work. Then another guy comes and makes the business a billion dollar enterprise with similar business idea.

Don't be the resistor: How to survive the longest in business?

While manufacturing Jetking radios, one of components used in the radios is called a resistor. A resistor is an electrical component that limits or regulates the flow of electrical current in an electronic circuit. Resistors are used to provide a specific voltage for an active device, such as the transistor.

Basically, a resistor controls the electric flow. If you were a radio, being a resistor would have been a good thing. But as an entrepreneur, being a resistor can be one of the biggest detrimental points in your growth.

If you get an idea as an entrepreneur and you stick with the idea, you won't last long because what your customers want is totally different.

There are movies where a person becomes so stubborn about his idea that he is not willing to change it. I'm not saying compromise on your values, but accept all changes that will come to your product as time goes on. One of the biggest mind-sets to have as an entrepreneur is that everything will change. Whatever thoughts you have about the perfect business will evolve and change and have 100 iterations based on customer feedback, and finally when the product comes to market, it will be very different from what you had imagined. You will also realise that the market is shifting so dramatically, you will have to keep changing your products from time to time just to stay evolved.

When Jetking was manufacturing radios, we were extremely successful in executing the production of radios. Then a change of market conditions resulted in high demand for the television. Although we obtained the government licences, we couldn't adapt to changing trends. Soon after that there was a huge wave of vocational training. We were able to adapt and grow extremely well. To the point we became the largest and the longest surviving player in this field. Today the whole trend is shifting online. Companies like Flipkart are getting valuations of billions of dollars. If you don't adapt to this change, you will be left behind. In fact, I have come to believe that every human being is very unique, so you have to change according to their way of understanding. Not to say you should compromise on your values. I used to eat a sandwich at Linking Road every evening after my work. Once I started getting piles, I had to change my lifestyle a bit. When I lost my father my whole life changed overnight. When I became a father, it brought about another change. People say it is difficult to change as you grow up. But I believe that the older you grow the easier it is to change, but only if you have practised and are comfortable with change. In fact, *Tony Buzan* has proven that your mind becomes sharper as you grow. The only condition is that you have to practice making it sharper every day. More than anything, change is a game of the mind.

There was a research done by a group of researchers to find a solution for stomach pains. They tried various formulas, and after months of trial and clinical research and testing, it was found not to be very effective. But one person sitting in the back saw that this medicine was creating a different effect. It caused a sensation in the penis, and thus Viagra was born. If the person had been a resistor, he wouldn't have seen that although the product for curing heart disease was a failure, it could be a revolution in solving certain sexual problems.

A very long time back in history, there was nothing on this Earth. Then, a single cell organism was formed. From it came multiple cell organisms (animals, etc.) These evolved into human beings. Over a long period of time, and through many ages, man kept on evolving, from ape to ultimately an extremely sophisticated human being of today.

As you can see, there was a constant change. Even in human history, nothing ever remained constant. The Roman Empire was built from nothing, yet it evolved into one of the most powerful empires to rule the world. Then it fell. The British, too, travelled the world, invaded and captured and ruled entire continents and ultimately lost everything.

The United States of America was a wild country. It was first occupied by the Native Americans, and then the British took over, and after a long conflict, ultimately had to leave. Today, the USA is the most powerful country in the world.

Take our very own India. At one point in history, it was the richest country in the world. The contributions that our ancient physicians, scientists, astrologers, etc. have made toward humankind have changed the entire map of human progress. For example, we gave the world the number '0'. Then India became a third world country, but it is now progressing so rapidly, it could very well become the most powerful and rich country all over again.

Even our bodies change. We are born, we grow up, we grow old and we die. Nothing remains constant. Change is something you cannot escape. But you can make it work for you or let it work against you. That's because we humans have the power of choice. We are not animals who cannot think rationally or don't have a choice.

You should start cultivating the art of flexibility, accept change rather than live in the past. We must realise that the same pattern that has got us to where we are will not get us to where we want to go.

One of the biggest challenge humans face today is that they resist change, justifying their actions by pointing out that their current behaviour is what got them to the level of success they now enjoy. This is absolutely true and, in reality, a new level of thinking is now required in order to experience a new level of personal and professional success.

I had gone for ten days Vipassana course lead by Mr. Goenka, one of the most influential teacher of this century. It was a mind boggling ten-day workshop. I actually experienced how my body is changing every second. How millions of cells are born and die every second.

Darwin's theory states the survival of the fittest is not the strongest or the most intelligent, but the one that adapts according to the situation.

The older I get, the more I realise that for every new situation there is a completely new set of characteristics, skills, mind-sets and sub-text. Responding to the new situation requires combining different skill sets in different ways.

For example, how I used to deal with my girlfriends will be very different from how I deal with my wife, which will be very different from how I deal with my son, which will be very different from how I deal with myself, which will be very different from how I deal with my employees. Even with employees, each one needs to be dealt as a very unique individual. So changing as per conditions becomes important.

Obviously there will be some similarities in the skillset I might use with a lot of relationships, but the quantity and quality of each skillset will be very different. However, I will have to customise myself to each individual to become successful with that individual.

It's important to see where your customers are located nowadays. As I write this book, most of Jetking's customers are on Facebook or outside college. They don't read newspapers any more.

First, we used to write receipts with a pen and make three copies of the receipts. One for the head office, one for the student and one for the franchisee. Today, all of it is software-based and you just take a print out and everything is done. I think in the future, things will further change to swiping your *Aadhaar* card and getting things done.

Second, my students used to learn through books and faculties. Today they find videos the most engaging. Slowly, students want fun along with learning. This is what I call infotainment. They want to learn while entertaining themselves.

I don't know if you know, but Instagram started off as a really complicated social application, but they pivoted. Here's a quote from their CEO and founder: "So, we actually got an entire version of *Burbn*, (which Instagram was called) created as an iPhone app but it was cluttered and overrun with features. It was really difficult to decide to start from scratch but we went out on a limb and basically cut everything in *Burbn* except for its photo and comment and like capabilities." That's it. What remained was Instagram. Recently, Instagram was sold to Facebook for a billion dollars. If they had stuck to it and not changed according to market need, they would not have been able to get the value they got.

Facebook started as a website to compare people, and today it's a completely different service.

If you don't have a mind-set of accepting changes you won't go far. Change allows you to embrace uncertainty, it allows you to embrace problems and it allows you to see the world as it's happening for you. This changes the attitude from the victim mentality to the attitude that I'm responsible for my creation in my life here.

9. *Being in a state of equanimity*, it's the ultimate state to be in. As the *Geeta* states, do your karma and don't be worried about the fruits. You keep taking action, and the result will come automatically. To do that you need to be in a state of equanimity, which means not getting affected by success or failure. Both should not go to your head. Both are temporary.

Mind-sets: Foundation of an Entrepreneur

योगस्थः कुरु कर्माणि
संगम त्यक्त्वा धनञ्जयः ॥
सिध्यसिध्योः समो भूत्वा
समत्वं योग उच्यते ॥ ४८ ॥

In Jetking, one of our core values is equanimity. I tell my sons that my ultimate goal is to reach a state of equanimity, where you are just observing all the sensations you go through as a human being, not getting attached or hating any of them.

Buddha achieved nirvana, the state of equanimity, or as they say in his language *anychya bhav*.

14. Coaching

As a businessman, we at times can't see the obvious things to do in the business. Has it ever happened to you that you speak to someone and they speak to you about their problem and you see that the solution is so obvious and it is common sense? But they don't get it. It's because they are caught up in their own emotions, ego, assumptions, etc. to see things clearly. You need to reach out to people to take your business to the next level.

In my study of successful people across the world, from *Sachin Tendulkar, Michael Jordan, Milkha Singh, Dhirubhai Ambani, Steve Jobs, Bill Gates,* you name a successful person, he is using the law of five. Some people might call it by a different name, like guru, teacher, or consultant. The more successful you become the more you require a guide who will move you toward your next level of evolution. Let's refer to this law of five as coaching. Entrepreneurs require this more than anyone, as this is a phase where an entrepreneur can walk on the wrong path, never to return. I have personally coached hundreds of entrepreneurs over the past few decades. I'm not saying you need to go with me, but you need a coach or several coaches.

Coaching is the fastest way to achieve result. I am yet to see a faster way.

Law of Five: (Connect to superstar reaching out to people)

Have you heard about the law of five? The law of five works on anyone and everyone irrespective of their gender, colour, religion, tribe, or height. It's a law. Just like the law of gravity, 'what goes up must come down,' this law cannot be argued with. It will work every single time.

If you have read the famous book Tribal Leadership by Dave Logan, he speaks about building a successful business like building a tribe. You need to build a tribe from people who you will consult or mastermind with, coach from, execute with the help of this tribe from time to time to take your business to the next level.

"A man can learn only in two ways, one by reading and the other by association with smarter people."

- Will Rogers

This law simply states that your business success is directly proportional to the five people you are closest to, and this law applies to everything like money, happiness, health, etc. So you want to do the math and see if this law is true? Calculate your net worth. Now estimate the net worth of the five people you are closest to. Add their net worth and divide by five. That will be your net worth. It's funny how that works, but it's a law. Similarly, if you want achieve the highest level of success, you have to associate and be friends with super successful people. They should be people who align with your success. This system will make sure that you understand and align your goals with this mastermind group to cut your rate of failure by 80% and speed up the process of achieving your goals ten times faster.

When I wanted to grow Jetking, I started associating with the best marketing consultants, quality consultants to advise me to get to the next level. Although it was expensive, it tripled my business.

Here is a short story I heard when I was a child. It's a silly story, but it makes the point.

Once upon a time, an injured eagle laid an egg on hay in a farm. She was so badly injured that she died before her egg hatched. When the little eaglet emerged from the egg, he was scared, alone and cold. There was no one to comfort him, give him food or keep him warm.

A hen passing by, heard the eaglet's pitiful squealing and came to see what was going on.

She was full of warm motherly love and compassion. When she realised the eaglet was an orphan, she immediately took him under her wings.

Time passed by. The eaglet grew up thinking the hen was his mom and the other chicks, his brothers and sisters.

One day, he happened to look up and what did he see? Beautiful, clear blue sky and very high above, a huge bird in the air. It was an eagle and how magnificent it was! It seemed to be totally still, was not even flapping its wings, just floating on the air currents. The eagle was obviously king, and the sky was his kingdom.

"That big bird looks exactly like me!" he exclaimed to his brothers and sisters. "I also want to glide in the air just like him!"

The chicks could not stop laughing at this. They said to him, "What? You are one of us. You eat with us, sleep with us, and play with us. We are your family. We don't fly - and nor can you!"

Utterly dejected, the eaglet hung his head and silently followed the chicks. He remained with his family for the rest of his life.

He never flew. Nor did he even try. What is the moral of the story? "You cannot soar like an eagle if you hang around with chicken and buzzards all the time."

Exercise:

Power of "Why." Superstars are driven. They create a strong reason for achieving their goals. Reasons that drive entrepreneurs range from making parents proud, buy a new home and so on. To succeed as an entrepreneur, you need to create a compelling reason that will constantly motivate and drive you. What are your compelling reasons for thinking about starting a business?

_____
_____
_____
_____
_____

Time management and daily disciplined action transforms a normal person into a super star who can achieve his goals and realise his dreams. Based on what you have learnt in this chapter about time management and daily disciplined action, which actions/activities will you start? Which activities will you stop? Which activities in your journey of becoming a successful entrepreneur will you continue?

Start _____
_____
_____

Stop _____
_____
_____

Continue _____
_____

CHAPTER 4

NICHE SELECTION

Part 1: What is the Niche?

As I've built my businesses over the past forty years, I've discovered a set of critical elements that must be done in order to succeed.

If you get all of these elements right, you'll be successful.

If you get even ONE of them wrong, it will lead to failure.

I call this the "Engine of Success." Imagine a car. Now imagine all of the things that must work in order for the car to work.

First, the battery must work. Then the engine must work. The transmission, the wheels and tyres, the electrical system, the gas pedal, the steering wheel and all the other components that make up a car must work. If any of these elements don't work, then the entire car doesn't work. I was reminded of this a few weeks ago when I returned from a trip out of town, and walked to my car, which was parked in the airport parking lot.

When I got inside, it wouldn't start.

My car has never had any sort of starting trouble.

The problem? The "vanity mirror" had been left open. And it had a small light in it. This light drained the battery. The car wouldn't start without a charged battery.

Are you starting to get the idea of what an "engine" is? Well get this. Your business has an engine for success as well. And if any of the key elements in the engine don't work, then just like the car...

...Your Entire Business Doesn't Work!

The first engine element of your business isn't mechanical at all. It's psychological.

As you've probably guessed, it's your niche. If you target the wrong niche, it's just like having a dead battery in your car.

The best motor and the nicest wheels can't take you anywhere if the battery doesn't start the car.

The nicest website with the hottest marketing in the world won't work if your niche doesn't work.

If you get the niche right, then it makes everything else you do in your business easier - and it makes everything else work better. EVERYTHING! If you get the business idea wrong, then it makes everything else hard - or even impossible - to succeed.

What exactly is a "Niche" anyway? Here is the Google definition of a niche:

A shallow recess, especially one in a wall to display a statue or other ornaments.

In my research, it seems that the word originally meant "a hollow or recess in a wall" - and possibly "a nest." In biology, they use the word to describe a place in a natural ecosystem where a particular animal or organism is perfectly suited and thrives.

Statues fill niches in walls. Animals fill niches in ecosystems. But, even more importantly...

...Products Fill Niches in Markets!

We might define a Market Niche as:

"**A need many people have, that your product fulfils.**"

Now, notice the change in mind-set this definition brings about.

It immediately helps you to realise that a niche isn't something you just "pick" from amongst a selection, like a song on iTunes. It shows you that a niche is something which must be found.

A niche must be discovered, uncovered and "solved."

The process of targeting a niche is about finding *a need that many people have, then creating or* finding *a product or service to solve it.*

One thing that stops people from even starting a business in the first place is their inability to "target a good niche."

I hear it all the time: "I'm having trouble deciding on a niche or a business idea." "I don't know which niche to go after." "I can't figure out which niche I want to market to." The "problem" with these problems? Simple! The problem is that if you start from one of these places...

...You'll Never Arrive at Success!

It's essentially impossible to achieve success selling products if you're trying to "decide" on a niche or "go after" a niche or "market to" a niche. If you're stuck trying to "decide" on a niche, then you're doing it all wrong. I don't mean to be critical here. I'm treating you the way I'd treat someone who was paying me sixteen lakhs as a franchise fee and 30% royalty. I'm telling you the truth, based on years of experience, mistakes and success.

Just as a niche is a hollow or recess in a wall, a good business niche is a "hollow or recess" in a group of people where one of their NEEDS isn't getting met.

The way to find needs that aren't being met isn't to "decide" which needs aren't getting met!

The way to find needs that aren't being met is to...

...Go and Find Them!

Let me share a story with you to explain this process a little better.

When my TV business shut down and I was looking for a new business, my consultant convinced me to start a training institute. I thought Jetking was known for radio manufacturing and so a lot of students would flock for training on manufacturing and repairing radios. To my surprise, my thinking was very different from reality, as I got very few students. So I visited colleges and talked to students to understand their needs. I realised that the main need of students was not to learn about radios but to get a job. I also realised that as a country, most Indians wanted to be either a doctor or an engineer, as these labels had great respect in the community at that time.

After speaking to students, I understood that their physical intelligence was stronger than their intellectual intelligence, and hardware engineering was more of a physical job where they had to repair and maintain a computer.

I thought there were so many computer engineers that there would not be any jobs for the hardware and computer engineers. So I went to my office in Lamington Road where I used to sell radios and spoke to several computer shop owners who were on the rise, and a few of my colleagues who had shifted to IT after their TV companies were shut down. I spoke to them to find out if they had any vacancies, and to my surprise most of them did. I asked them, since there were so many computer engineers in India, why they didn't hire a computer engineer? They told me that most of them were software engineers and they required hardware engineers – yet no college was teaching computer hardware and networking. I realised by speaking to students and recruiters that there was a huge gap in the education system. The university and college had a syllabus that was not relevant to the industry. There was a massive demand for IT engineers. Technology changed so fast that there was no way a university could keep up with it. The approval process in a university takes a very long time and by the time the changes are approved, technology has changed again.

Also, the salaries of engineering graduates were very high and they could not afford such engineers. So I asked them how they were fulfilling this requirement, and they said they were hiring non-technical students and giving them on-the-job training.

I saw an opportunity here and I gave all my students who enrolled, a 100% job guarantee, on a stamp paper because I had so many vacancies. After that there was no turning back. Similarly, there were many such vacancies across the country because for every fifty computers sold, you required a hardware engineer to maintain them. So I thought of opening an IT training franchise which would in turn solve the problem of these computer shops and IT companies who manage computers.

Today we give our students access to over 12,000 recruiters across the world.

What's the moral of the story?

The moral is simple: If you want to target niches successfully and dramatically increase your chances of success, you need to find out what people need - and don't get.

Then, find or create products and services to fill or solve their needs.

Remember when I mentioned the "engine" to a successful business? Well, this is the FIRST STEP on that critical path.

If you get your niche wrong, there's no way to fix it. You can work for years trying to create the right product, the right marketing, or whatever. But if you don't get the niche right in the first place, you are, as they say, a "failure."

You'll spin your wheels, waste time and money, and be generally frustrated trying to figure out why your business isn't working if you get your niche wrong.

If you get your niche right, half of your work is done.

When you get your niche right, everything becomes much easier. Marketing works better. Customers come out of the woodwork. Other businesses want to partner with you to sell your products.

All the stars line up!

Narrow Your Niche

What I'm about to tell you next is one of the hardest things to "get" when it comes to targeting a money-making niche.

It's hard to get because it's literally the opposite of what the mind normally does when considering a business niche or product idea.

When you're starting a business or creating a new product, the "intuitive" thing to do is try to make it appealing to as many people as possible.

"Widen the market appeal," as they say.

It only makes sense to try to make your business and product attractive to as many people as possible, right?

Well, it's almost right. Except that it's actually...

...*Totally and Completely Wrong!*

What could be wrong with making a product that lots of people want?

You're probably thinking: "You've lost me now. Are you suggesting that I make products that nobody wants?"

It's a fair question - especially considering that, what I am saying sounds preposterous.

So here's an experimental thought:

Let's say that you have a headache, and you decide to go down to the drugstore to get some medicine.

You walk over to the aisle filled with all types of pain relievers... and then choose one of them for your headache.

The question is:

What did you choose? And why?

If you're like most people, you would choose Crocin - a medicine that's marketed specifically to cure fever and headaches - or something similar.

Now, stop for a minute and imagine that you're standing there looking at the pain relieving medicines, and you happen to look up on the top shelf... and see a big blue bottle of pills that's labelled...

"Medicine."

Would you buy it?

Would you even pick up the bottle to read it? Of course not.

A bottle of pills labelled "Medicine" sounds about as interesting as a menu in a restaurant where everything is labelled "Food."

Why? Why don't we want the thing that "cures everything?" Well, it turns out that we humans aren't exactly logical.

In fact, modern science is proving more and more that we're "Predictably Irrational" (the title of Harvard professor *Dan Ariely*'s book about the topic).

In other words, we behave in irrational ways - but we're predictable in our Yes! We do crazy things. We don't know why we're doing them. They're consistent and predictable. We make up stories in our minds to rationalise and explain them, rather than just noticing that what we're doing is driven by "animal drives" and emotions.

One of the less than logical things we do consistently is buy things that sound like they were made to fix our specific problem (or give us our desire) - and avoid things that sound like they "cure everything" or "fix whatever is ailing you."

So now you're starting to see why widening your niche to include a bigger audience is a problem. Instead of focusing on a targeted group of people that has a strong need, widening your audience causes you to create a medicine that nobody wants to buy.

Which brings me back to my point: If you want to really target a potent niche that will be likely to make you a lot of money, then narrow your niche, don't widen it. Repeat after me:

"Narrow My Niche."

The first step in creating a niche is to understand your own strength and what you are perceived as credible amongst a target market.

If you're an expert at helping people lose weight, and you've discovered that there are lots of women who want to lose ten kilos fast because they're getting married and want to look great in their wedding dress, then FOCUS on them.

Don't write a book on "health." Write a book for the women who want to lose weight for their wedding!

If you're an expert helping people get out of debt, and you do a survey and discover that the biggest frustration with debt is high credit card payments, then create a product about (you guessed it) how to get rid of high credit card debts.

Don't create a product about "achieving financial security." Got it? Narrow your niche. Narrow your niche!

Narrow it based on the part of the niche that causes the most frustration, worry, pain or desire. This way you're creating a product that is really desired.

The Ultimate Niche Shortcut: "The Big three Mega-Niches" as David Ogilvy said,

> "A blind pig can sometimes find a truffle. But it helps to
> know that they're found in oak forests."

As it turns out, most of the money that's made in information products, advising, consulting and coaching is made within a few key "mega-niches." If you know what these are, it can give you a big head start over everyone else, and get you far down the path of targeting your money-making information product niche (or your next product).

If you've heard me teach on this topic, then you know what these three mega-niches are:

1. Health and Fitness
2. Dating and Relationships
3. Business and Money

In fact, if you look at all of the "big hits" in information products, probably 80%–90% of them are within one of these categories.

What I'm trying to say here is that if you're targeting a niche, and you're looking for a big frustration or need you can fill with your product or service, then start there.

Now, as you can tell, these are very "wide niches" indeed.

You don't want to create a product called "health and fitness."

But you do want to start within the mega-niche of health and fitness. What do you do next?

You narrow your niche by figuring out what a specific group of people who are interested in health and fitness are looking for, but can't find.

When I started my training institute, I started off in a broad category, teaching a lot of famous vocational subjects because I thought I would get everyone to join and make a lot of money.

But that's not how customers think. Business owners want to satisfy everyone, but customers want a customised service.

At that time, I looked around at the marketplace and realised that there were a large number of institutes teaching most of these vocational subjects. So my consultant, niche master, *Zafar Khan* suggested that I narrow my niche to one thing. At that time NIIT and Aptech had captured the software market and I was too small an institute to compete with these giants. There were not many jobs available in electronics and radio. The late Rajiv Gandhi had introduced computers at that point in time and just like there is now, there were large number of vacancies coming up in IT hardware and networking.

I didn't want to narrow it down because I was thinking about all the students I would be leaving out, but fortunately *Zafar Khan* was persistent and late in the night we decided to shut everything else and focus solely on hardware and networking. And the rest, as they say, is history.

I narrowed the niche from technical vocational courses to IT courses and finally narrowed it down further to hardware and networking.

At that point in time I eliminated 98% of the technical vocational market. What was the result? I created the world's largest hardware and networking training company in just a few years.

Is this making sense to you?

Just like you'd choose a medicine specifically created to cure headaches and not "medicine," a person who has a specific challenge or desire wants an information product that was made specifically to solve that challenge or need.

The basic idea here is to start with one of the big three mega-niches, then narrow your niche within that mega-niche by discovering a big need that isn't being met well for a large group of people.

If you do this, you'll increase your chances of success even more. Stack all of these techniques and approaches I've shown you, and you'll find a winner.

Your Information Product Niche Cheat-Sheet

As you can imagine, in the past twenty-six years of building successful information product businesses, I've discovered many niches that are "high probability" winners.

I'd like to share with you what I consider to be the biggest gold mine opportunities inside the big three mega-niches.

I'll share each of them with you, then explain why I think each is a good short-term and long-term niche business opportunity - and then show you how to find the "bull's eye" within the niche that you would like to work with.

This list has taken me a long time to compile and understand, and I hope you use what you learn when you study it to profit from your business.

NOTE: I am not a doctor, attorney, or government employee. I am not giving you legal, medical or business advice here. If you decide to pursue any of the categories that I'm about to mention, it's your responsibility, and it's up to you to get legal, medical and professional advice. It's also up to you to follow the law of the land for your business and marketing. And with that disclaimer, let's look at where the opportunity lies...

Health and Fitness

1. Natural Weight Loss

It's useful to follow long-term trends when choosing a niche. Both "natural" and "weight loss" are long-term trends, and they're meeting up now in the niche called "Natural Weight Loss." As a society, we're becoming more and more concerned about chemicals, drugs and other elements hurting us more than helping us. Natural weight loss is growing fast and will continue to grow long into the future. A few examples of this are VLCC, *Pooja Makhija*, *Rujuta Divekar* and *Sarita Davre*, to name a few experts.

2. Stress

One of the "penalties" of living in a world that's changing faster and faster is the average person's inability to handle change. Relationships are changing, families are breaking down, job length is shortening, and debt is increasing. It all leads to more stress. All this is creating a huge opportunity to generate products and services to reduce it and make it go away. Thai spas nowadays are mushrooming everywhere to solve this problem, there are counsellors to reduce stress, and people who teach meditation come in this niche too.

3. Muscle Gain

The other side of "weight loss" is muscle gain. The two are not the same. In fact, someone who wants to lose weight may not want to gain any muscle. And someone who wants to gain muscle may actually want to gain weight (muscle weighs more than fat, after all). If you've been watching infomercials on TV over the past couple of decades, then you've seen the rise of the "Muscle Gain" niche. It's a big winner, and my bet is that it will continue to win long-term. Gyms like Gold's Gym, True Fitness, etc. help you achieve this. Protein drinks, personal gym trainers, and books on this topic are examples for this niche.

4. Low-Impact Exercise

As the health benefits of exercise continue to be explored by science (and realised by individuals who integrate exercise) and the health "hazards" of "hard core military exercise" are coming to light, people are looking for alternatives that offer them the benefits of exercise without the risks. An entire industry is sprouting around the category of exercises that give you benefit but don't hurt the body. People who teach yoga come into this niche.

5. Fat Loss

As a testament to the power of narrowing your niche, we're seeing an entire category of weight loss emerging right now. It's the "Fat Loss" category. So what's the difference between weight loss and fat loss? Nothing, probably. But as research is showing that increased

body fat (especially around the abdomen) increases risks for all kinds of nasty diseases, something interesting is happening: Fat is becoming "the enemy." It's literally being demonised. And this is leading to a new "niche within a niche" called fat loss. It's a good one! *Pooja Makhija, Rujuta Divekar* and *Sarita Davre* again come into this category.

6. Organic Food

Fears of genetically modified foods, along with dangerous pesticides and other chemicals, are leading to a huge trend towards organic food. This is leading to a growing interest in organic food; where to procure it, how to prepare organic food, and the benefits of organic food. It's a fast-growing category of interest that promises to give us many successful "narrow niches" in the future. Godrej has opened stores in metros by the name of Nature's Basket and Foodhall by *Kishore Biyani*, which are doing extremely well.

7. Raw Food

Within the categories of natural and organic foods is a relatively new, fast-growing category called "raw food." Raw food restaurants are popping up all over the world. The benefits of raw food - from energy to beauty to health - are being proclaimed, and everyone from celebrities to mothers are getting into it. Even I like to eat a lot of raw food. I see this category growing long into the future. A great niche opportunity. Books on growing your own organic food are in demand. At *Pali* Market near where I live, along with regular vegetable vendors who sell their vegetables in that market, there is a lady who has a stall to sell raw organic food. She sells her products at a premium to other vegetable vendors and by the end of the day she is sold out.

8. Natural Healing

Alternative health and healing isn't exactly new anymore, but it's picking up the momentum of a freight train. It's sub-divided into all kinds of interesting different niches - and creating huge opportunity for a lot of entrepreneurs. People are losing their faith and trust in western and allopathic medicines day by day and they're turning to alternative "natural" methods. *Baba Ramdev* is one of the best examples for this.

9. Wellness

I typically avoid "prevention" categories, as most people aren't searching for "prevention." Those who are searching for it have no sense of urgency around it. So it is difficult to create a successful business here. But the "wellness" category is a little bit different. As the self-help and personal development gurus are teaching us to get in touch with how we're feeling in our bodies, many of us are realising that we feel bad - and that we'd like to feel good. In other words, we want to realise our full "wellness potential." Increasing health, energy and vitality is becoming a big business, and you can do well in this category if you choose a motivated group of people to create solutions for.

10. Any Specific Health Problem

This area is "sticky," as it's often illegal to sell or market specific "cures" to health problems (again, check with your lawyer). But the fact is that when someone has a specific health challenge, they become very motivated to get an education about that particular topic. If you can create an information product that helps people solve a specific health problem quickly, you can become very successful - while at the same time creating a lot of value for people who are in pain.

Relationships and Dating (Including Parenting)

1. Dating

I think this is a great category and niche. We come "pre-wired" at birth to grow up and seek a mate, and the first step to getting a mate is to get a date. Men and women are both highly motivated to learn how to successfully date and to attract a partner - and dating is going to be a successful category for as long as humans are walking around on the planet.

2. Relationships

If the dating goes well, then the real challenges begin. Successful relationships require communication skills, partnering skills, teamwork and myriad other skills. Relationship advice will also be a successful information product category in the long-term, and if you have experience or expertise helping people have successful relationships, then this is a great way to "do well by doing good."

3. Marriage Counselling

The ultimate "relationship" is, of course, marriage. Marriage can be thought of as a category within the relationship category. But marriage is special because it carries the implications of "lifetime commitment." When people get married, they enter a new phase of their lives, and many things change. Finances, responsibilities, and stress become more complicated. As you probably know, marriages are failing at an alarming rate, and helping people have successful marriages is a great place to target your niche.

4. Sexuality

Every single one of us is here on this planet as a result of, you guessed it, sex. I think sex is at the root of more negative emotions than almost anyone could guess. Fear, anxiety, guilt, shame, jealousy, and many other emotions result from our personal and cultural relationship to sex. If you can help people have a more fulfilling sex life, you can do very well for yourself in information marketing.

5. Conflict

The intersection of "pain" and "urgency" usually offers great opportunity to create information products that sell. The general area of "conflict" is an excellent place to start "hunting" for a niche that needs your advice. Whether it is relationship conflicts or family conflicts, these are the areas where people get the feeling that they need help often - because they intuitively know that if they experience too much conflict, the relationship will end. If you can help people who are having family and relationship conflicts, you have what it takes to build a successful information business in this category.

6. Divorce

The "ultimate" relationship conflict is, of course, divorce. It has its own section in some bookstores. An entire army of lawyers focus only on divorce law. Big money is at stake when divorce comes into the picture, and if you can help people with this level of relationship conflict, then you have a huge amount of natural, "built-in" customers for the long-term.

7. Body Language

I've listed body language here in the "Relationships and Dating" section, but the truth is that it's a topic that "crosses over" to all three mega-niches. We want to learn to read body language to flirt with and attract a mate. We want to learn to read body language so we can persuade and sell better, and change our own to communicate our confidence, health and success. In every case, it's a category that's growing in interest and success right now.

8. Parenting

I typically don't advise that information marketers target niches that have to do with "prevention," as it's much harder to market and sell products that are "preventive." But when it comes to kids, the game changes. People will do anything for their kids. But most people don't know what to do, especially if they have a child who is misbehaving, or has a learning disability, or who is socially awkward and self-conscious. Parents are spending more and more money on their kids and on learning how to be good parents. It's another niche that's going to be good for the long-term...or at least as long as we continue having children!

9. Education

This is really a "sub-category" within parenting - in a way. Parents are starting to think about how their six-year-old is going to get into Harvard, and are starting "accelerated education" courses for their children at younger and younger ages. Everything from education games to education videos - and everything in between - is becoming a very big business. If you know how to help parents educate their kids for long-term success in life, then find an unmet need in parents and create inf ormation products for it!

Business and Money

1. Real Estate

Even though real estate business booms and busts, it tends to always be a good category for products. In fact, it can often be even better when the market is bad - because when the market is good, people don't think they need help! Real estate investment is complex, multifaceted, and interesting. There are many niche opportunities within this massive category - and if you have experience making money or creating a successful business in real estate, this can be a very profitable category to work within.

2. Foreign Currency

The Forex market (short for Foreign Exchange), in my opinion, has become the new-day trading. It's a high-risk, high-energy game where big money can be made or lost in seconds. That's probably why so many people are getting involved in it. It's also something that basically anyone can get involved with if they have access to some money and a computer - its popularity is growing fast. If you have knowledge of how to make profit in this market, you should consider teaching others what you've learnt in the form of products.

3. Investing

In India, we're saving and investing less and less of our money. But all that's changing as the economy goes through its ups and downs. Investing is a "counter-intuitive" skill. Humans like to spend what they get for instant gratification. If you have investment knowledge, there are many niche possibilities for you to test and explore.

4. Retirement

Lately, more and more people are realising that old-age is coming, and retirement accounts don't grow themselves. As I mentioned in the "Investing" section, we've been saving less and less, and the sombre realisation that retirement requires money is dawning across the land. If you can teach people how to successfully retire (or how to deal with the challenging aspects of retirement) you have a high probability of creating a successful information business. Retirement is a long-term opportunity, as the entire population is only growing larger and getting older!

5. Debt

You already know that people are taking on more and more debt. The problems that come from having too much debt, lead people to seek solutions with great enthusiasm. I personally think that debt is one of the biggest challenges we face as a society, and if you can help people get out of debt and build healthy financial habits, then you owe it to yourself to test this category with a product.

6. Starting a Business

The Internet is creating a massive wave of opportunity for literally anyone to start a business from home. Millions of people are working part-time and full-time from home, running an eBay business alone. Whether it's an Internet business or a traditional business, people who are starting their own business need help. Business has many twists and turns, and there's not enough good "Starting a Business" advice in the world today. There are so many niche opportunities within this category (and so many more created every day with new inventions and technologies) that this category will never run dry. This book belongs to this niche.

7. Making Money

I hesitate to even mention this category because so many products sold in this niche are garbage - or scams. The fact is that if you ask people what they need right now more than anything, a large percentage of them will answer "money." As it turns out, making money is harder than it would seem. If you can help people get started on making money (honestly, of course!) then you should test a product on the topic.

8. Marketing (Especially Online)

In business, everyone is trying to get more customers. It's the high priority activity for most businesses. If you ask 100 business owners who failed in business and went bankrupt what the "problem" was, most of them would answer "not enough customers" in one way or another. What's the best way to get customers? Marketing! Marketing is great, because it allows you to focus on your core activity and the marketing does the work for you. Advertisements run day and night in magazines, on TV and online - without a person there to do the selling. And I'll tell you from experience, if you can teach people how to market their businesses successfully, then you can create a big win in this product space.

NOTE: Online marketing is one of the biggest opportunities that will come along in our lifetimes, so if you can learn it and teach it, you really have an opportunity to do well.

9. Time Management

What's the big enemy of business success in modern times? It's distraction and interruption. As I mentioned in the earlier chapters, I've discovered that time management is one of the biggest challenges that business people and entrepreneurs face. And I think this is one of the big "unseen opportunities" to create successful products now and in the future.

10. Getting a Job

The latest estimates are that the average college graduate is going to have something like a dozen different jobs and several entire career changes before the age of thirty-eight. Think about that. And since most people will be working for a business during this period of their lives, one of the key skills to have is knowing how to get a job in the first place. If you know how to write resumes, interview like a pro or network to get good job interviews, then you should consider launching a product in this category. Jetking has mastered this category.

Pradhan Mantri Kaushal Vikas Yojana is a unique initiative by the Government of India that aims to offer Indian youth meaningful, industry relevant, skill-based training. Under this scheme, the trainees will be offered a financial reward and a government certification on successful completion of training and assessment, which will help them in securing a job for a better future. To support the government's vision, Jetking has set itself a target to help make one crore youth employable and get jobs by 2020. There is a huge opportunity in this sector. I say this from experience, no matter how many people join this sector, there is room for more. The biggest challenge in this niche at this point in time is not employment but employability and motivating students to take the jobs where there are vacancies. Because most students are not in touch with reality and they have big aspirations to get a job which involves sitting in an air-conditioned cabin, and working behind a desk. If anyone can fulfill this need, you are most welcome to partner with Jetking. If not, you can start your own business, too.

So There You Have It...

Twenty-nine powerful niche market opportunities that sell tons of products right now, and will work long into the future.

So what should you do now? You might answer, "Pick one and create a product." And if you did answer like that, I'd say: NO! Remember what we learnt earlier?

Remember the part about "narrow your niche?"

If you'd like to pursue one of the twenty-nine niches I mentioned above, you should identify the specific area where you'd like to sell products (or advice or coaching), and then narrow that niche to find a specific part of that niche where there are people looking for a solution, and no products are readily available.

For example, let's say you decide you want to teach marketing. Further, let's say you've been learning and practising social media marketing online for yourself and a few friends or customers, and you can see that there aren't many good products that teach social media marketing.

What you would want to do is start a discussion group inside your favourite social networking site or just ask all of your friends/followers a question:

"What's the biggest challenge or frustration you're having with social media marketing right now?"

Then start reading the answers!

You'll start to see patterns, connect the dots, and see opportunities for niches that you hadn't thought of before.

You might discover that the biggest frustration is turning followers into customers, or it might be getting followers or friends in the first place, or getting people to visit your website.

What I've discovered is that when you ask, you always end up being surprised at the responses you receive. This is where the opportunity lies. Because when you start with a niche that already makes money, narrow that niche by finding an unmet need within, you discover an opportunity to take your own knowledge or expertise and create a product that's unique - and valuable - to many people.

The twenty-nine niches I gave you were more than sufficient to start deep diving and getting into a business of your liking. In case something didn't resonate within you, below is a list of industries from which you can choose.

Personally, I prefer to come up with my own market ideas, but this may be helpful for you.

1. Accountants
2. Air Conditioning
3. Architects
4. Attorneys
5. Automotive Service & Repair
6. Bankruptcies
7. Brake Service
8. Car Dealers
9. Car Rental
10. Carpenters
11. Carpet Cleaners

12. Carpet Laying & Repair
13. Chiropractors
14. Computers
15. Contact Lenses
16. Contractors
17. Counsellors
18. Day Spas
19. Dentists
20. Electricians
21. Employment
22. Fence building
23. Flooring
24. Hardware
25. Heating
26. Home Improvement
27. House Cleaners
28. Insurance
29. Kitchen Cabinets
30. Kitchen Re-modelling
31. Landscape Gardeners
32. Lawn Mowers
33. Limousines
34. Martial Arts
35. Massage Services
36. Mortgage Brokers
37. Movers
38. Opticians
39. Optometrists
40. Painting
41. Pest Control
42. Photographers
43. Physicians
44. Plastic Surgeons

45. Plumbers
46. Printers
47. Real Estate Agents
48. Restaurants
49. Roofing
50. Security
51. Siding
52. Sprinklers
53. Travel Agencies
54. Truck Leasing
55. Veterinarians
56. Window Installers
57. Breweries
58. SaaS (Software As A Service)

Filtering your business ideas

Deciding on a profitable idea can be tough and confusing at times. This section will help you choose the most profitable idea that has the least chance of failure.

Good niches start with emotional needs that people are having - which are then used as an inspiration to create great products and services to solve them. Use my "Niche Assessment" to filter each of your niche ideas, and discover which ones are worth pursuing and testing. The test is simple and it can save you an amazing amount of time and money.

Here's how to use it:

1. Ask the six questions below when considering a niche.
2. If you get four "Yes" answers, then you've got a good niche idea, and you should test it.
3. If you don't get four "Yes" answers, keep tweaking your niche idea until you DO. Use the niche test every time you're planning to launch a new product or business to dramatically increase your chances of success.

These are guidelines, so some of it may or may not apply to you.

Before you choose a market idea, it is important to decide the sector you are targeting: different sectors have different criteria and here are the three main sectors:

1. **Consumer:** We will start with criteria for consumers:
    1. Does he want to solve his problem now?
    2. Is he pro-actively seeking help?
    3. Are there a few or many competitors? (fewer the better)
    4. Is he experiencing pain when he is not solving the problem?
    5. Is solving that problem one of your strengths? If not, do you know someone who can solve that problem? (get into partnership/employ him)
    6. Is he willing to pay upfront? (use this with responsibility) You are here to solve a problem not dupe people, so if you cannot solve the problem don't take the money. It's different for different people; some people want to create a product and then ask for it, I want to understand the pain and frustration, understand if I have the capability to solve the problem, and if so I will take the money first then solve his problem.
    7. Does it appeal to beginners? (There are lot more beginners that will go for your service than expert level services.)
    8. Is your business idea in the growth, mature, or dying stage of that particular industry? Radio manufacturing was once upon a time an industry in the growth stage. Today it is almost dead since mobile phones have an in-built radio. Mobile apps are in the growth stage, user interface technology is in the growth phase, profits are at a maximum in this stage, while the automotive industry is a matured industry so the profits are not very high. It is ideal to target an industry which will be growing for the next three to five years.
    9. Are they motivated by fear or desire? (Fear is twice as motivating as desire.)
    10. Is the revenue recurring? In my opinion it should be at least for twelve months, you want a customer for a long time because it's more expensive to get a new customer. Thus, it's better to have a customer pay you for a longer period of time.
    11. Is there at least 1 in 1,000 people looking for this solution?

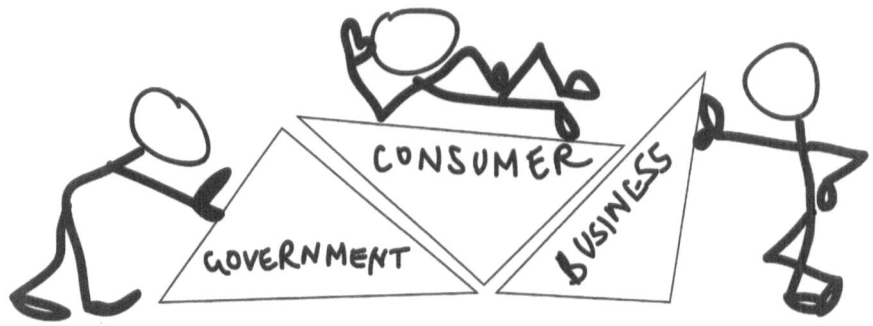

2. **Business:** For business, the criteria are simple.

   No. 1

   The business currently pays for similar kind of service or solution.

   No. 2

   Lucrative industries are preferred.

   No. 3

   Profit driven business mind-set.

   No. 4

   Roughly 5,000 to 10,000 businesses (or more) in the market.

   No. 5

   Reachable by phone, email, Facebook, LinkedIn, Twitter, or message boards.

   No. 6

   Can get person with pain point on the phone.

   No. 7

   The average successful business earns at least rupees one crore per year in revenue, and ideally, profit.

3. **Government:**

   My recommendation is to stay away from the government sector because it is a different animal. You will have to invest first and then get the return in any government project. There are many rules and criteria set by the government that helps them get more votes which might not be beneficial to you as an entrepreneur. For the majority of my career I have stayed away from the government. There is a saying, "Long live the queen," but stay away from the queen. If in any case you want to do business with the government, you must treat it as a business sector and make sure they meet those criteria, otherwise don't get in to it.

Part 2 How to find the most profitable business idea?

The Go and find them When deciding on Niche three most important things are considered.

Every person on this planet has come with extremely unique ability to perform certain tasks. They are sent on this planet earth with very specific unique set of skills. Your job as an entrepreneur is to find that unique set of skills and just keep doing that activity which comes very naturally to you and you enjoy it and work seems like play when you are doing it.

There is a book called One thing and the author is *Gary Keller* and Jay Papasan.

In that book the author says that just focus on one thing you are really good at everything else will come to you automatically name, fame, health, money.

It is important to recognise your awesomeness. Society conditions have messed up our minds, schools have messed us up even more, where all students are being taught the same subject without understanding what the student is good at. The school system was introduced during the industrial era to make factory workers. They wanted people to enter into the factory at nine and leave at five and keep doing same job over and over again.

They were expected to just answer question go according to norm, not to talk to their neighbour. Today we are in the 21st century. If we do not talk to our neighbours we would be out of a job. The course-school system is not relevant any more.

It is your birth right to know what makes you brilliant.

People get into drugs, alcohol and bad habits because they are not living a life of awesomeness - their true calling.

So let us try to find out what is your awesomeness is. What do you love/enjoy doing?

_____
_____
_____

What are your values?

_____
_____
_____

What is your core strength?

_____
_____
_____

What is the one thing you are really good at and keep doing even if you didn't get paid for it?

_____
_____
_____

What is something you are really bad at?

_____
_____
_____

The next step - Amazing Accurate Audience

One of the most important misunderstood concepts in business to which, say is critical to crafting promotional material in a way that feels good to great to every potential client and will get an effective result.

Bear in mind amazing accurate audience is the same which you really care about.

When trying to choose an audience you want to serve to, it is important that you go for people you really care about because that will come through your selling.

One big mistake most Professionals make is they want to make a product that will cater to an audience from the age of two to the age of eighty. But the fact remains people do not buy in the similar manner.

They would buy a product or service which would speak to them directly. So you want to focus on that target group, generally about 5 years of age, to where you were and the challenges you faced and the way you overcome challenges.

So target audience should be narrowed down from 5 years to 10 years. Now amazing accurate audience is pride label to it.

Pride Label is something that a person relates to and feels proud about.

EXAMPLE: "Mother"

What would happen if I went up to a mother, and told her she wasn't a mother?? She'd be confused at first, then mad – then indignant!

Say Mother is an amazing accurate audience is going more narrow.

EXAMPLE: "Teacher"

People who work in teaching profession would put their hand up and say, "Yes! I identify with that label. I am a teacher."

When you choose a strong Egoic label to identify your amazing accurate audience, and you use that label in your marketing, you will get a similar reaction. A person will pick up your brochure, read your ad or see the announcement for your speaking engagement and they will say, "Wow! This is a sign from God! This was written just for me!"

Even in teachers i.e. amazing accurate audience what would be a more accurate audience either primary school teacher, secondary school or a corporate trainer or sports. All these four audiences have different needs and need different services.

Following are some Pride Label you can narrow in on:

RELIGIOUS:
JEWISH
MUSLIM
CHRISTIAN
ATHEIST
BUDDHIST
MORMON

RELATIONSHIP:
MOTHER
GRANDMA
SINGLE
MARRIED
FATHER
DAUGHTER

PERSONAL:
VEGAN
NON-SMOKER

OWNERSHIP:
HOME OWNER
DOG OWNER
RENTER
HONDA OWNER
MAC OWNER

VOCATION:
ENTREPRENEUR
CHEF
SMALL BUSINESS OWNER
PROFESSIONAL WOMAN
CAREER COUNSELLOR
HIGH SCHOOL STUDENT
NATUROPATH
HIGH SCHOOL TEACHER
PLUMBER

NATIONALITY:
AMERICAN
CANADIAN

GENDER:
(ADD TO OTHER LABELS):
FEMALE
MALE
WOMAN

HOBBY:
YOGINI
RUNNER
SKIER

Exercise:

Amazing accurate audience Factors

What are their values?

Maybe they are like you 5 years ago. Where are they in their lives now? What do they love? What do they fear?

Name
Age
Gender
Occupation
Income Level
Education Level
Family Information
Other Relevant Information

My Amazing Accurate Audience is:

(Name Your Audience by Pride Label)

Particular Painful PROBLEM

What is a Particular Painful Problem?

"A Particular Painful Problem is the clearly defined, precisely determined problem you solve for your Amazing Accurate Audience." Again, in this case, I'm referring to the problem you'll solve FIRST for your Amazing Accurate Audience.

The first thing to understand is this - You are an entrepreneur! And here is my definition of an entrepreneur. "You solve Problems for People at a Profit."

To build a successful business, people must strongly desire to give you their money. People won't hand you money because of something you can do.

People won't give you money because of some skill you have, or something you are good at. Nobody cares about that.

Only reason someone will give you their hard earned money is because they have a problem...

...And they think YOU can solve it!

This is why you need to be crystal clear about the problem you are solving in your marketing.

Again, it is about SELF SELECTING.

You would want your client to see your marketing and say, "I have that exact problem. This is for me."

If you are fuzzy at all – they will overlook your marketing.

There are 3 STEPS to get clear on your Particular Painful Problem. Are you ready?

STEP 1 is to write down your SOLUTION.

Three Mega-Niches

The three mega-niches are as follows:

- a. Health and fitness
- b. Dating and relationships
- c. Business and money

Examples of Niches

Finance: share market: equities for investor: futures and options:

Business: startups: accounting for startups: sales for startups: Facebook marketing for startups the more you niche out the better

Niches

Health and Fitness

1. Natural Weight Loss
2. Muscle Gain
3. Stress
4. Low-Impact Exercise
5. Fat Loss
6. Organic Food

7. Raw Food
8. Natural Healing
9. Wellness

Any other Specific Health Problem

Relationship and Dating

- Dating
- Relationships
- Marriage
- Sexuality
- Conflict
- Divorce
- Body
- Language
- Parenting
- Education

Business and Money

- Real Estate
- Foreign
- Currency
- Investing
- Retirement
- Debt
- Starting a Business
- Making Money
- Marketing (Especially Online)
- Time Management!
- Getting a Job

_____
_____
_____
_____
_____
_____

STEP 2 in identifying your PROBLEM

People will not come to you when they have a problem. They will come to you when they have a Particular Painful Problem.

Pain is twice as motivating as fear Convert Solution into a Problem you'll phrase your problem as what I call, a 'Particularly painful Problem.'

People don't need a solution when they are in pain. They need a solution when pain becomes unbearable.. So if you have normal pain would you go to a doctor… No!.. You would go to a doctor when the pain is unbearable

So unbearable particular painful problem Health: headache, fat, thin, tired, wrinkles Wealth: cash flow, investing, not enough clients

Relationship: fighting with boss, teens not listening

Sex: not getting any, low libido

Identity: not being a very good X (Egoic Label)

_____
_____
_____
_____
_____
_____

Particular Painful Problem

Health	
Overworked	Aging
Too busy	Looking older than your are
Exhausted	Headaches
Overwhelmed	Back pain
Burn out	Stressed
Overweight	Hot flashes
Chronic stomach pain	Infertility
Bloating	Acne
Bladder infection	Eczema
Addiction to sex	Depression
Pulled in a million directions	
Chronically sick	
Sleepless nights	
Wealth	
Not knowing what to do with my money	
Revenue rollercoaster	
Stuck @5 or 6 figures	
Worried about retirement	
Inconsistent cash flow	
Revenue plateau	
Paying too much tax	
Overspending	
High debt load	
Not knowing how to invest $$	
Finances out of control	
Not enough clients	
Not keeping clients long term	
Worried never be able to buy	

Relationship	
Fighting with spouse	Feeling disconnected
Alone or lonely	Unsupported
Not being understood	Kids or teens pulling away

Parenting	
Kids grades	Bullying
Kids rebelling	Teens doing drugs or alcohol
Kids not listening	Fighting with kids
Lack of commitment	

Identity	Sex
Hating my job	Not getting any sex
Stuck on 9–5	Low libido
Dreading work	Bad sex
Complaining wife	Sex addiction
Bossy dad	Erectile dysfunction
Unapprochable boss	Not feeling sexually compatible with partner
Passed up for promotion	No passion
Bad friends	Feeling unattractive
No career direction	
Not being taken seriously	

Example 1: Here's how a POSTURE THERAPIST may do the steps.

I help Amazing Accurate Audience improve their posture. [Solution]

I help amazing accurate audience with bad posture [Solution phrased as problem]

I help amazing accurate audience with lower back pain [Problem phrased as particular painful problem]

Example 2: RELATIONSHIP COACH

I help my Amazing Accurate Audience create fantastic relationships [Solution]

I help my amazing accurate audience with relationships that aren't working [Solution phrased as problem]

I help my amazing accurate audience with their fighting and arguing. [Problem phrased as particular painful problem]

Example 3: NUTRITIONIST

I help my Amazing Accurate Audience increase their energy [Solution]

I help my amazing accurate audience overcome low energy. [Solution phrased as problem]

I help my amazing accurate audience with feeling tired all the time. [Problem as particular painful problem]

___
___
___

Identifying the niche is critical for the success of any business. Study the various business ideas listed in the chapter and identify five business ideas that appeal to you the most. List them out in order of importance, your strengths, and immediate customers you can sell your products to. You can also include your own ideas.

___
___
___

People will pay for the solution that will make the pain go away. It is important that you narrow down your niche, based on the actual information rather than your assumption. To narrow down the niche in the business ideas that you have shortlisted earlier, you should speak with people and identify the pain they are experiencing. Speak with five people for each of the idea and list the pain they are seeking the solution for.

___
___
___

CHAPTER 5

GETTING THE BUSINESS MODEL RIGHT

Now that you have the business idea, you really have one incredibly urgent job: To get into profit! And the only way to get into profit is to get the value equation right for your business.

The business model will determine the kind of business you'll have, how easy it will be to get new customers, and how fast you'll grow. You've got the business model right when your customers are happy to pay you more than it costs you to deliver value to them, because the value they are getting is much greater than the price they are paying to you. Simply put,

VALUE > PRICE > COST

For example, if you are starting a wedding photography business. Your business model is the value that people place on getting their wedding pictures taken, at say Rs. 5000, which is more than what you would normally charge them to do the job; which is around Rs. 2500, which in turn is more than what it costs you to take their pictures and deliver them in a manner that satisfies the desired value, which is say at Rs. 1500.

Rs. 5000 > Rs. 2500 > Rs. 1500

Of course, it's not enough to know how much a customer values wedding photography. Your true business model is based on how much your customer values wedding photos taken by you. This is why every entrepreneur must find their own business model. You can follow general guidelines created by the others in your field, but ultimately your value equation is yours alone.

(If You Don't Know) Where to Begin

If you have no idea what your business model is, start with thinking of the offer that you could make to a customer. For now, focus on just two parts of an offer: the benefit or promise and the method or process to deliver the benefit.

Examples of well-formed offers:

I will help you lose weight (promise) by offering telephone coaching (process).

I will save you time in your email inbox (promise) by offering you a software that organises it automatically (process).

I will offer you low cost alternative energy (promise) by installing solar panels on your roof (process).

I will give you an alternative to radiation therapy (promise) by giving you rare herbal mixtures with healing properties (process).

Notice that we've removed all the superlatives and marketing hype here. These offers are specific, easy to understand, and relate to. For the purposes of understanding your value equation, you should avoid offers like these:

I will facilitate a transformational experience of whole new possibilities.

(Too vague!)

I will help you get to the next level in your business.

(Better, but still too vague)

I will offer you a suit that will make women love you.

(Exaggeration!)

I will add Rs. 50 lakhs to your profits by making sure your website doesn't break.

(Process not credible to keep promise.)

I offer a completely different kind of coaching that nobody else does.

(There's No Promise, Only a Process!)

It's like quora.com for plumbers, but with Uber's business model.

(This Isn't Even an Offer – What Benefit Is the Customer Getting?)

Write down your offer. Then read it back and compare it to the examples of "well-formed" offers and "poorly-formed" offers. Which group does it most closely resemble? Keep narrowing it down until it sounds and feels just like the other well-formed offers.

Once you've settled on the promise and the process you're offering, you can start to find out how customers value what you've got and how much it will cost you to provide it.

Now you're on a scavenger hunt, looking for all the different people that want to take advantage of your offer, ways you could make good on the promise, and all the different ways you could deliver it.

What Customers Want? What It Costs You to Deliver? What Customers Will Pay?

In each of the above questions, there are points that do not overlap with the other. Customers are willing to pay for parking tickets – even though they don't want them. You can afford to offer a small bag of rocks to your customers, but they don't want to pay for that and they don't want it either.

There is also a world of products and services that customers want, but are not willing to pay for. Most people want a full-time gourmet chef, but less than 0.01% of the people are willing to pay for it. Most people want to fly private jets rather than commercial. Most men want a movie theatre in their homes. Most women want a 1000 sq. ft. shoe closet. But again, very, very few are willing to pay for them. Even many of those that could technically afford these things are unwilling to justify their costs.

Based on this, it is not enough to ask a potential customer if they want what you have to offer. You also have to know if they value it enough to buy it.

How Do You Measure What Someone Else Values?

Have you ever had a salesperson ask you, "How valuable would it be to you to solve this problem?" You probably have difficulty coming up with a good answer to that question because it causes a conflict in your mind. Let's say you wanted to buy a cast for your broken arm. If the doctor asked you, "How valuable is it to you to be able to use your arm again?" Of course, it's priceless! But does that mean you are willing to pay all the money you have for that cast? No, of course not.

It can be challenging enough to discern exactly what value you place on different products, services, and experiences. Add to that, the differences in how different people see the world and approach their lives and you can imagine the challenges of understanding what someone else values. So how can you measure it?

Customer Value Interview Script

1. What is the main value you expect to get from my offer?
2. What price would you be unwilling to pay for this offer because it's too high?
3. What is the lowest price at which you would still rather keep your money than get the benefit of the promise?
4. What would you pay to another company for a similar offer?
5. Would you pay more than the offer of the other company or less than that to me in exchange for my offer (and why)?
6. What is the highest price that buying this offer would occur to you as a 'no brainer'?

7. What are some ways I could change my offer to make its value more tangible to you?

Here are a few questions that are easier to answer than the classic salesperson's approach and give you a lot better sense of how your potential customers value your offer. Talk to people who are qualified to be your customer and explain your offer to them. Then ask them these questions.

This can be a sobering conversation or an enlightening one, or both. We recommend talking to at least ten customers and recording the conversation. The exact words the customer uses to talk about their situation are valuable for marketing and copy writing key words and phrases, and you will often hear important things when you listen back to the recording that you missed in the moment.

Once you've interviewed ten people who are qualified to be your customers about what rupee figure they attach to the kind of promise and process you plan to offer, you will begin to see a pattern of different people saying the same kinds of numbers. The 'value' variable in the value equation is the average of the answers to the *Qn. No. 3* The 'price' variable in the value equation is somewhere between the average answer to *Qn. No. 4* and *Qn. No. 6*.

Change Your Offer to Lower Risk

Increasing the customer's perception of the value of your offer dramatically increases your flexibility and chances of success. Higher the value, the more options you have on the cost side and more freedom to charge a higher price.

During your ten interviews, you'll notice that changing something about the process often dramatically changes the perception of value, even though the promise hasn't changed.

That's because customers automatically build in risk (or their assumptions about the chances of success) into their own sense of value. For example, which is more valuable, Rs. 100 cash or a lottery ticket with a chance to win Rs. 100,000,000? You chose the cash (hopefully!) because you are automatically building into your assumption the fact that the lottery ticket isn't very likely to succeed.

Your customers do the same thing when they consider your offer – which is why they value the same offer from different companies and entrepreneurs so differently.

Think about how your customers view the chance of success with your product or service. What are the things that you could do to change your promise or process that would lower the risk of failure and increase the chance of success in the customer's mind before they purchase? Those ideas are going to help you solve your value equation.

Once you have arrived at the value your customer gets from your offer, you've anchored the solution to your value equation on one end.

$$KNOWN\ VALUE > PRICE > COST$$

Calculating Your Costs: The Basics

To understand the importance of cost, let me explain how it impacted our TV project. When Jetking got the licence to manufacture TVs, we were extremely happy that the government gave us the licence and we were the chosen ones to get the licence. We didn't calculate any of the cost of manufacturing TVs and just went out and took a loan.

If I ask you to think of the cost of TV raw materials, like the motherboard, tube and cabinet, which cost Rs. 8000, and you have to manufacture 1000 TVs, how much money will you require? If you are able to reply, you are good at finance, however when I ask this question to many people they are not able to calculate it in their mind. Similarly, on the human resources front, we did not take into account the availability of engineers and the cost of relocating them to *Lonavala*. Sales was not a problem, but human resource and finance were the two things we did not factor into the equation. The cost of infrastructure and TV motherboards escalated beyond control. Further, we did not factor in the corruption at various levels. The State Bank of India sanctioned just forty lakh rupees and this sabotaged our project in the early stages. By the time we realised this in 1989, the interest and principal amounted to Rs. 76 lakhs. We went to Canara Bank and submitted the project; they took their own sweet time and disbursed the loan slowly. Also we took hand-loans of around Rs. 1 crore, so our loan burden grew to Rs. 3 crores. By the time we realised the problem, 6 years had passed and we could sell only 300 TVs. The whole project turned out to be a non-starter. Slowly, TV manufacturers, due to tough competition, started falling like a pack of cards. By rough estimate, only three companies called Videocon, Onida and BPL survived. The next area to investigate is your cost. For your business to be successful, include all the expenses required to deliver value to the customers according to your offer.

There are different categories of cost, which we'll cover in order of most obvious first.

Direct Costs – expenses you pay out of pocket in order to deliver the value of your offer. If you own a restaurant, the cost of all the ingredients that went into making the meal that the customer bought is the direct cost. If you run a carpet cleaning business, then the hourly wage of the employee while they are on the jobsite with the customer is a direct cost. Direct costs are variable, because they go up when you have more customers. Some businesses, like coaching, have no direct costs at all.

Allocated Costs – expenses that are related to your business but aren't direct. Overhead expenses such as your accountant, equipment leases, and printer paper are often allocated costs.

As the name suggests, in order to figure out how much it costs you to provide your service, you have to allocate some portion of these costs to each customer. This can be a bit tricky, especially in the beginning, because it's hard to know how many customers you are going to have.

If a software company spends Rs. 25 lakhs developing its software, and expects to have twenty-five lakh customers, then it can allocate Rs. 1 per customer in allocated costs. But if they guess wrongly and end up with only 100,000 customers, suddenly they have Rs. 10 in allocated cost, which is dangerous when you were counting on only Rs. 1.

In the beginning, assume a 50% utilisation rate and calculate your allocated costs based on that assumption. If you are a massage therapist, the maximum number of clients you can take is likely three to four massages per day, five days a week. Twenty massages. That would be 100% utilisation. 50% utilisation would be half of that, or ten massages per week. Then you can add up all your allocated expenses for the year, say Rs. 10,000. If you work forty weeks per year, that's 400 massages. Rs. 10,000 per year divided by 400 massages is Rs. 25. That means you have Rs. 25 per massage in allocated costs.

Here's the formula one more time:

Allocated cost per customer = Total Yearly Allocated Costs/((Max Per Week * 50%) * Work Weeks)

Now you have direct costs and allocated costs, but there is a third category of costs, which is the most important and the most often overlooked. In fact, it is this third category of costs that is most often responsible for the failure of a business.

You Messed Up Your Numbers: Miscalculating Cost

The third category of costs is hidden costs, which are almost never calculated by start-up entrepreneurs, leading to miscalculation of costs and getting the value equation wrong.

Hidden costs are the costs it would take to run the business without you, your assets, and your special relationships. They are not paid in cash, which is why they are so often missed. The largest cost for most startups is the hidden costs of the salary of the founder. Since the founder rarely takes a salary, it's easy to miss, but you don't want to go without a salary forever, and if your value equation breaks when you add in the cost of what you want to get paid, then you'll never get out of the start-up phase.

That's how some businesses that have been around for decades are still in the start-up phase – they haven't calculated the hidden costs, so the founder is still working at way below the market rate for their contribution to the business.

If you imagine having to pay someone else to do your job, how much would you have to pay to ensure that you could get someone who is capable of doing a good job? If your business relies on the fact that you own land, or your brother is doing you a favour, or that cousin Phil is willing to work for nothing, it is very important you count these hidden costs, allocate them as if they were indirect costs, and add them into your value equation.

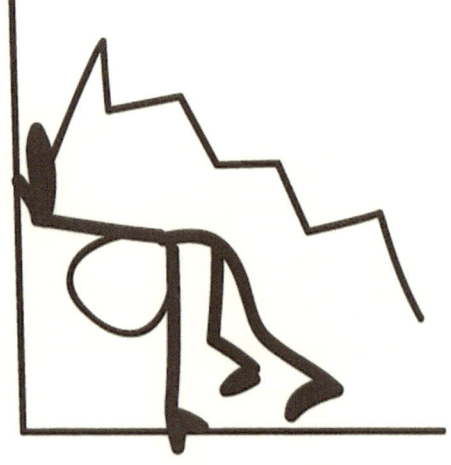

To finalize the cost variable in your value equation, add the direct costs, and then figure out how much allocated cost to attribute to each customer. Then calculate your replacement salary and the rest of your hidden costs. Add the three together and you have the true picture of what it costs to deliver your value to the customer.

In a web design business, you might have a direct cost of Rs. 1800 to get someone to help build your client's website, allocated cost of Rs. 300 for your equipment, overheads, etc. And hidden costs of Rs. 150,000 per year or Rs. 1500 per website developed (assuming ten websites per month). That's a total cost of Rs. 3600. If you can charge Rs. 3600 or more per website, then you have found the solution to your value equation.

Total Costs = Direct Cost Per Customer+ Allocated Cost (Total Divided By 50% of Max Utilisation) + Hidden Costs (Total Divided By 50% of Max Utilisation)

Sadly, most entrepreneurs don't make this calculation. It would be an easy mistake to think, "It costs me Rs. 1,800 to get the website done. If I charge Rs. 3,000 I'm making good money on each one." That's true until you take into account your hidden costs, and then you realise that in fact you are losing money on each website, not making 'good' money at all.

More than likely, the first time you calculate your costs they are going to come out higher than your price. Almost every business in the start-up phase starts that way. You can temporarily make the business work by taking less money for yourself, but over time that strategy will take its toll on you and you'll start to feel imprisoned by the fact that you never solved your business model.

That means you have to innovate and iterate over time to drive your costs down and the value you are providing. That's why the most important focus you can have in a start-up business is understanding the business model and getting it right.

The more you separate the direct and the hidden cost, drive the value up and bring the costs down, the better the business you will create. Your business will grow quickly, creating more value for customers and in turn more cash for you.

The Price is Right, Isn't It?

Once you know the value and the cost, then you can place your price point anywhere in between and be safe. But how do you know where in between to place your price?

Pricing is as much an art as a science, to get started, consider profit margin versus sales velocity.

Profit margin is how much money you make in profit on every sale. All other things being equal, the more you charge for your product, the more profit you make.

But all things are not equal, and one of them is sales velocity, which is the speed at which you meet and convert new customers. In the corporate world, a Rs. 250,000 consulting project could take dozens of hours in exploratory meetings over the course of six months to turn it from an idea into a sale, whereas a Rs. 3,000 strategic software purchase can be approved in a thirty minute phone call. How many thirty minute phone calls could you have in six months? It would only take fourteen calls per month selling the Rs. 3,000 software to be more profitable than the Rs. 250,000 consulting project. That's because of sales velocity.

Lowering your price doesn't always increase sales velocity, but it often helps. Experiment with different pricing models to get the right price point.

When I started my Jetking School of Electronic Technology, I charged Rs. 12000 and at that point in time, I got only five students in two months. As inquiries came in I realised that people were finding it expensive, so I slashed the price by 50% based on the conversation I had with my consultant. I enrolled 160 students in two months and there was no turning back.

Cash Always Tells the Truth

Your customer may not know what they would buy and what they wouldn't buy until the time arises to do so. They also may know but not wish to share. Interviewing potential customers is crucial to getting your value equation right, but pay more attention to what customers say with their time and money than what they say verbally.

Your customer's spending habits will tell you what they really value and in what proportion. That's why you're not out of the start-up phase and into sustainability until you've not just created your business model in theory, but demonstrated it.

When you have around ten to twenty customers who have all bought roughly the same thing from you for roughly the same price, and they are ecstatically happy with the value they've received from your products and services, then you're into sustainability.

Exercise:

A business idea remains an idea unless it is backed by an offer for the customers. A good offer is the one that states the benefit your product or service offers to the customer and the process that you will follow to deliver that benefit. An offer should not exaggerate the value and the process should be credible. When creating an offer for your idea, write down the offer statements and refine till you get a perfect one. In the space below, write down the offer statement for your business idea. You can use another sheet of paper to practice statements and write the final statement in the space below.

_____
_____
_____
_____

Getting the cost correct is very critical for the success of your business. The costs can be broadly classified into direct costs and indirect costs. For your business idea to fructify, write down the direct and indirect cost that you will have to incur.

_____
_____
_____
_____

Entrepreneurs need to get a good understanding of the value the customers associate with your product or service. More often than not, entrepreneurs make the mistake of overestimating or underestimating the value the customer associate with the product or the service offered. Speak with ten potential customers, using the customer value interview script, to get an idea of the value customers associate with your product or service. In the space below, write down the price (average) the customers are willing to pay you.

_____
_____
_____
_____

CHAPTER 6

HOW TO GET YOUR FIRST 10 CUSTOMERS

There are three guaranteed steps to find constant current of clients.
1. Collect leads of your Amazing Accurate Audience with niche sitting.
2. Give them lot of value through massive moolah based marketing
3. Respectfully Do super sexy sales.

Steps to start selling your service to the amazing accurate audience is to find where your Niche is sitting. For eg. our students are sitting in Jetking and our clients are sitting at three primary places: Colleges, Online, Google and Facebook.

So here are the different places where a Niche can be found.

Online

- Blogs (free or cheap)
- Facebook ads (cheap)
- Instagram (free or cheap)
- Book my show (cheap)
- You Tube (free or cheap)
- Facebook groups (free)
- Meetup.com (cheap)
- Coupon websites (cheap)

Offline

- Vistage (vistage.com)
- Speed Networking Seminars and Workshops
- Newspaper (expensive)
- Colleges (free or cheap)
- Radios (expensive)
- Hospitals (free or cheap)
- BNI (free or cheap)
- Training programs (free or cheap)
- Chambers of Commerce
- Relationship Building Network
- Small Business Expositions
- Small Business Meetup.com Groups Speed Networking Events
- Television (very expensive)
- Networking events (free or cheap)
- bus hoarding (expensive)
- Networking events
- Meet ups (free or cheap)
- Meets (free or cheap)
- Business Network International
- Lions Club International

Top Ten List Building Activities

- Set up a Social Media Profile.
- Post a link to your giveaway on your Social Media Sites.
- Join or Start a Meet-up Group.
- Attend a Live Networking Event.
- Join an online Forum for your niche.
- Get Booked to Speak.
- Write and post on an article distribution site.
- Identify 5 JV partners.
- Reach out to JV Partners.
- Create a Pay-Per-Click or a Facebook Campaign.

Kindly identify top five online and offline places where your Niche is sitting.

3% = ACTIVE

7% = OPEN to buying your stuff, not actively shopping.

30% = AWARE they'll need you in the future.

30% = UNCONSCIOUS

30% = NO!!!

One of the best ways to collect leads is to provide high value to your Niche.

Once you have collected the leads, you need to provide high value to your customer before doing actual sales.

To understand value kindly refer to chapter two titled Customer Resonance. I will tell you how we provide value to our prospective clients in Jetking.

Once we have collected the leads we call them for free workshop on computer assembling and disassembling. We also do an assessment of the students to understand their strengths and weaknesses.

We also help students do their goal setting since most of the students are confused about their career. When we give this module for free, massive value trust and respect is created in the eyes of the prospective client. Jetking is perceived as a high value brand because of this experience.

So below is a diagram which tells you what needs to be given for free.

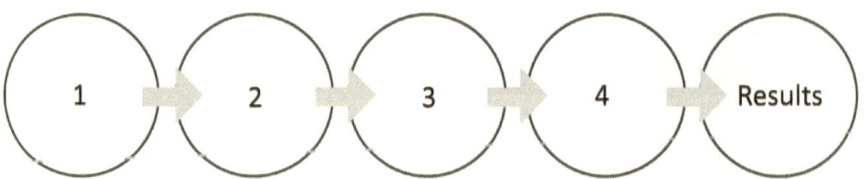

So a person requires to do four steps to reach the required results.

So you offer or give the first step for free. Once he has experienced your brand product or service he will trust it and hence he is more likely to buy it from you at a premium price.

One of the highly successful businessmen I met gives away more than 80% of his service for free and charges 10X as compared to the competition and is very successful. If you trust your product or service and you believe that it will help your prospective clients reach a particular result and you give away 10% or 20% of the product for free, it will build massive credibility, trust, respect for your product. Another advantage of giving away so much value for free is that your contribution to the society for free will eventually come back to you in some form or the other.

Giving value is the most EFFECTIVE because,

- It sets you up as a Trusted Adviser
- It gives you an Authority (helps you charge a premium).

Value is the only marketing strategy that works – for small businesses anyway. There are other ways to market.

You could spend tons of money and do BRAND Advertising like Kraft, McDonalds and Coke. But I've found most small business owners don't have the money for that.

The coolest part about Value is you are building your brand, offering value and changing the world through marketing.

Exercise:

Right now imagine all of your Amazing Accurate Audience.

These people have the problem you solve and are dying for your program, product or service. What is a free value you can offer them?

Once you have offered them value you need to pitch them your product or service and convert them into clients. So, what is Sales?

The exchange of a commodity for money; the action of selling something.

The process of seeing whether my product fits the client's needs.

Do you know the oldest profession in the world? Whenever I ask this to my audience, they tell me it is prostitution. But even that is selling. Selling is the oldest profession. Everything you do is selling and everything you don't do is also selling.

Why is sales important?

It's the last mile.

Gets customer to take out the money and create goodwill. Gets the customer fully committed to the product.

Handles objections. Charge premium prices. What are the ramifications of not selling?

You will not be able to grow your business. You will not be able to charge premium. You will not be able to make the customer buy in the way they love.

How is sales done?

1. One on one (live or phone). It is suggested to start with this as it is the cheapest and cost effective.
2. Through workshop.
3. Full-fledged online sales.

Depending on your niche and you can blend the above. It is recommended you start with this, as this is by far cheapest and cost effective way you can do through workshop and call Amazing Accurate Audience.

What is the Sales devil telling you?

India is an introvert country. Traditionally every person in India either wants to be a doctor or an engineer. A majority of the people do not like to sell because they are perceived as low value, greedy person who is just here to take money from the clients pocket and put it in their own. But that is just social conditioning talking. If you come from a place of love, respect and giving value then sales becomes one of the most enjoyable and fun part of the business. One of the misconceptions people have is that selling is bad. You need to ask yourself what you will benefit more, from selling you as an entrepreneur or a prospective client?

If the answer is you as an entrepreneur, then you are not selling at all. If your answer is your client, it will benefit more than you from doing the sale. That is the time you are ready for sales. If you understand that concept of sales you will understand that at the end of the day considering your product is right and your Niche has a need for this product. Eventually a certain number of people will buy from you. So what are the few successful mind-sets of the top salesman. One is believe that after doing sales the prospective client will love you more. Believe that you are selling you are giving and not taking. Believe that this product is the best thing that can happen to your prospective client. Believe that the person will eventually buy from you. Believe that his life will change after using your product/service that sales is a fun process and not this scary rejection prone devil. Now before you are doing your sales there are certain voices in your head which stops you from selling and giving your 100%.

Some of the things that come up in your mind are:

What if I'm too pushy or what if I'm not too pushy? What if I am rejected?

What if I get disrespected?

What if the client does not have time and money?

What if the client takes me as a BPO call centre executive?

If these voices helped you in getting your sales and income and the lifestyle you want I would say retain these voices and continue living like the way you are but you and I both know that these voices will stop you from doing that sales giving that 100% and living the lifestyle you always dreamed or desire.

What will make you money or what will get the client is having the belief and the mind-set of the top salesman. So finish off all negative voices on your head and come from the place of strength, love and respect. Next time you are pitching your product or service to your prospective client, instead of asking yourself, if he will buy your product, ask yourself if he is the right client.

Most often people don't take action because of fear of rejection. We are living in 2017 which is probably the safest time in the history of human civilisation.

During the "hunters-gatherers" era, majority of the people would not know that they would be awake by morning or be eaten by a wolf or bear. Even if some animal would not eat them they would die of some common disease like fever, mosquito bite, malaria etc.

Today you just have to hear a "no" from the prospective client. There are certain parts in the world like Somalia where people do not survive past their youth and their hands get cut off, heads being cut off if they are not obeying their leader. Majority of my clients are scared to call or pitch because they are scared that the prospect will hang up on them or tell them they do not have money or time or make them feel like a call centre executive.

Sales for me is more about finding out if the client is right for my product/service and I am verifying my client all the time to make sure he fits my "Amazing Accurate Audience."

At the end of the day if I am talking to ten clients everyday and I speak to 100 clients in ten days and even if 99% rejects me, I still make one client every ten days. Based on the lifestyle and the goals you want you might just need 5–10 clients in the whole year to achieve your goals. So even if I get one client every ten days, at the end of the year I have thirty-six clients which is a good number.

If you are not feeling well and you go to a doctor and the doctor prescribes you medicine, does he sell you about how supercool or awesome the medicine is and all the benefits the medicine has? No. He just tells you to have this medicine twice for the next three days and you will be alright because he knows that his medicine works and he cares for you.

Second example: If a child tries to put his hand into boiling water what would you tell him? You would try to stop the child or even shout at him to make sure he does not touch the hot water again. So are these mind-sets coming from a point of manipulation or caring?

As a sales person you need to have a mind-set of a doctor or caring parent who wants his client or his child to be safe and grow.

You have to understand that in sales everything might be for sale but not your self-respect. At the end of the day you are only one and they are many. Even if they pay you Rs. 5 lacs for an hour, self-respect is still not for sale.

Sales as a disqualification process.

Your main job in sales is not to find out if the person will buy. The main job is to get rid of people who will not fit your "Amazing Accurate Audience" and your product/service. So the shift in the mind-set is that you go from being a mushy soft and fearful guy to an assertive sort of guy who decides whether this person is suitable for you versus I am scared, I hope this person buys this product. If you see any company, business has been successful because they have a selection criteria.

Fear vs Love

I need to pay my rent, need to take a vacation, desperation.

vs

I need to sell with love and self-respect and see if he fits.
Closing someone without giving value is desperation.
I want to close this person quickly and get on with the next.

vs

I want to take my time and see whether this person fits in my clients list.
I want this person's money.

vs

Does this person qualify to be my client?

It is important to have a strong mind-set around sales. One way is to push people, cajole people, lying to people to buy the product. Another step is to choose people who would fit your product/service and do it with self-respect, love, authenticity and care.

Fear based selling says that I will be selling, anything I can with lies and manipulation. And love based selling says I am here to provide a value at least ten times more value than what I will charge. Sales is not manipulation, and sales is not accepting every sales.

Following are the questions which will help a person get into a buying state and ready to buy a product when you pitch it.

Goals and What They Mean/What They Are Worth

1. Tell me a little bit about yourself (or if you are a business coach, "tell me a little bit about your business", of if you are a relationship coach, "tell me a little bit about your relationship", etc.)
2. If you could wave a realistic magic wand, where would you like (your business, relationship, health, etc.) to be in the next six months to a year?
3. If you had that in just the way that you'd like to have it, what would that do for you?

4. What would be the best part about it?
5. Why?

Challenges and Their Impact

6. What do you think could be slowing you down, standing in the way, or stopping you from having all of this? (list their goals from Question 2)
7. What else do you think could be slowing you down, standing in the way, or stopping you? (Repeat until they don't have anything)
8. What impact do you think these challenges are having on your (business, relationship, etc.)?
9. What impact are these challenges having in other areas of your life?
10. How long have these challenges been going on for?
11. What's the worst part about these challenges?
12. Why?
13. The Turn-Around/Light at the End of the Tunnel.
14. If you could turn all these challenges around and flow freely towards your goals, what would that do for you?
15. What would be the best part about that?
16. Why?
17. What have you found most valuable about our time together so far?
18. I have a programme designed specifically to help people overcome these sorts of challenges and achieve these kinds of results.
    Would you like to hear a little bit about it?

How You Help Them

19. Explain how your coaching works (use the five part coaching methodology & relate it back to their goals & challenges)
20. Check in to see if they are with you –"Does this make sense?" "Would that be valuable to you?"
21. Explain your fees ($XXX/month, $YYY/Full Pay, etc.)
22. Which of these options feel like the best fit for you?
23. Would you like to give it a try?
24. Great. Let me get you entered into the system. If someone isn't ready to move forward now, help them overcome their fear and see if they are ready to move forward after that.
25. Once you have pitched your product they will come up with objection.

Objection Handling

PHASE ONE	PHASE TWO
Actively listen	Remind
Reward Reassure	Realign
	Reframe with sale story

PHASE THREE	PHASE FOUR
Contrast/Future pace	Trial close until you feel they are ready

PHASE FIVE

Hard close for Credit Card

Objection Handling

PHASE ONE _____

1. ACTIVELY LISTEN and then raise the objection back to them: "So I hear you saying"

2. REWARD them for sharing the concern to make them feel good about being open: "Thank you so much for being honest and sharing that with me, because we like to begin our relationships based on the truth -- you're going to do well!"

3. REASSURE them that their concern is common and easily overcome "Actually you'd be surprised MANY of our IDEAL clients come to us with EXACTLY that same concern and it ends up being THE reason they join us!"

PHASE TWO _____

4. REMIND them of why they asked for help in the first place and reconsolidate the value: "REMIND me though, before when we first began the conversation you were saying you really wanted to_____ correct?"

5. REFRAME them with a sales story, either of a client or from your company's achievements. It could even be a well-known historical anecdote. Begin with the hero being where they are now. The middle should be the hero taking the decision they need to take. The end should be the hero winning. The MORAL is always WHY they need to make the choice to buy.

PHASE THREE

6. CONTRAST. You need to dig in and show them the contrasting value they are missing out on at the moment. Draw the contrast to show them what they're leaving on the table when they don't buy. "So you have two choices: 1. You can remain stuck and not able to do what you want (use as much of their personal info and language as possible from your information gathering) and 2. You can make the choice to do something about it and get (all the things they said they wanted) so which are YOU going to be?"

7. FUTURE PACE them - take them forward and show them the negative effect of not choosing you. Alternatively, FUTURE PACE them - take them forward and show them the positive of choosing you.

PHASE FOUR

8. TRIAL CLOSE.

    "So If I could get you that result would it be worth taking a small step forward and starting that process?" "So how does that sound?" "So what would that feel like if it was twelve months from now and you HAD that result?"

PHASE FIVE

9. HARD CLOSE: Visa or MasterCard

    You are now ready to start a business and make some money and start getting clients. The most important component now is how fast the execution would be. Majority of people think and talk a lot from, if you go out and execute. Execution changes everything. It converts poor to rich people. It converts dreams in to reality. So my hope is that you will got out and execute and turn your dream into reality.

Timeline of Suresh G. Bharwani

History

1953	Birth of *Suresh Bharwani*.
1958	Enrolled in Saint Theresa High School, *Bandra*.
1961	Failed in 3rd Standard.
1962	Shifted to *Kamla* High School (Sindhi Medium) because understanding topics taught in English was difficult.
1966	Stood first in class, got double promotion.
1970	Completed SSC with distinction.
1970–74	Joined *Sydenham* College, one of the best colleges in Mumbai for Commerce and Economics.
1970–74	Studied and simultaneously visited Lamington Road shop. Authored a colourful and graphical sixteen page *"Do it Yourself"* manual for pocket transistor, where irrespective of any technical knowledge one could make radios with own hands.
1974	Started Radio manufacturing unit in a 500 sq. feet workshop in Tardeo, Mumbai (1 Feb 1974).
1978	Shifted the transistor factory to a spacious 4000 square feet area in Bussa Industrial Estate, *Sewri*. Capacity to manufacture one lakh radios per year with state of art R&D facility (8th April 1978).
1982	Started a small factory to manufacture TVs in *Milan* Industrial Estate, Mumbai.
1983	Public Issue – Certificate of Incorporation (26 Dec 1978).
1984	Started TV Manufacturing unit in Lonavala.
1989	Closed down Factory in Lonavala with heavy losses.

1990	27th March 1990 – Launched Jetking School of Electronic Technology by *Hashu Advani*, Finance Minister, of Govt. of Maharashtra Partnership.
1997	Joined hands with Novell. with Microsoft and International Correspondence School, USA.
2004	Jetking ranked as leading Computer Hardware and Networking Training Institute by Dataquest Magazine, one of India's leading IT publication.
2005	The Government of Maharashtra awards Jetking with "Maharashtra IT Manpower Development Award'.
2006	Jetking was awarded "Hall of Fame" award for ground breaking effort in the world of Indian franchising by Franchising India Holdings Ltd.
2006	Ranked 4th in the list of twenty-six Hot franchisees as per Outlook Money magazine.
2007	Awarded "Pike's Peak" Award by The Bob Pike Group, an International Performance Solution organisation for successfully evolving a Creative Training Technique to deliver technical training in a fun, faster and easier way.
2008	Launched Heathkit Omni Firm to make troubleshooting training easier.
2009	Launched JetEgde – Powerful English Speaking and Softskills Training programme.
2012	Recipient of the Limca Book of Records for students placement across India. Launched centre in Vietnam.
2014	Jetking Infotrain Ltd awarded as India's most trusted brand in Computer Hardware and Networking Training by Brand Trust. Felicitated with FICCI Leapvault Skills champion of India award for its extra ordinary contribution to the skill development in India
2015	Jetking launches. "JETKING ONLINE SCHOOL OF TECHNOLOGY." The first E-Learning platform in IT & IMS.
2017	Suresh launches a book close to his heart. THE ENTREPRENUER's GUIDEBOOK.

www.ingramcontent.com/pod-product-compliance
Lightning Source LLC
Chambersburg PA
CBHW031922240526
45464CB00021B/632